CONQUERING THE ODDS

Turn Your Valley Into

A Mountain Top

HABIBO HAJI, RN-BSN

TABLE OF CONTENTS

Chapter 1

TEEN PARENTS

"Nothing you become will disappoint me; I have no preconception that I'd like to see you be or do. I have no desire to foresee you, only to discover you. You can't disappoint me."
— Mary Haskell

"My mission in life is not merely to survive, but to thrive; and to do so with some passion, some compassion, some humor, and some style." —Maya Angelou

"You may encounter many defeats, but you must not be defeated. In fact, it may be necessary to encounter the defeats, so you can know who you are, what you can rise from, how you can still come out of it." — Maya Angelou

"Every adversity, every failure, every heartache carries with it the seed of an equal or greater benefit." – Napoleon Hill

---

For fourteen years, my grandmother, Halima, was the only mother I ever knew. In fact, I called her Hoyo, which means "mother" in Somali. As a baby,

I slept with her on her filiq, a mat woven from grass and each day she'd carry me on her back using a long morro (a piece of cloth tied in the front) while she walked the goats and sheep through the grasslands to graze. She did this every day until I was three and too heavy for her to carry.

Grandma always fed me with milk gotten from one of her goats or cows while she herded them. I remember rubbing her feet when I was older because they were always worn out from walking the animals. She never ceased to tell me how easy it was for her to take care of me.

My father was nineteen when he married my mother who was few years younger than he was. Their marriage was arranged by their fathers even before they both met. Their fathers thought it would be a good idea for them to stay within the family since they were from the same tribe which makes it easier to get along with the relatives.

After they married, they moved to the big city of Mogadishu. And my mother got pregnant with me. She told me the story of when I was born. My father and his mother took her to the hospital in the afternoon, where she was told that she couldn't leave until the next day. At that time, the hospitals did not provide food for the patients; their family had to provide meals. Unfortunately for my mother, no one brought her food. She was left there alone to give birth to her first child. She labored all night and finally had me in the morning. My father arrived in the morning and asked at the desk what the sex of the baby was. He left when he was told my mum was delivered of a baby girl. He didn't even go in to see her or bring her anything to eat or drink. Later that afternoon, he came back to the hospital to take us home. Shortly after, they got a divorce. My mother went to live with her father when she was unable to take care of herself. My grandfather was delighted to have my mother come back home, as she could help take care of his children, along with her new baby. It seemed like a good arrangement except for the fact that my grandfather had a short temper and was violent towards those around him. My mother told me how difficult it was to take care of me and her siblings. She had no time for herself, and taking care of the boys was a challenge for her. It was difficult for her to assume the roles of being a mother, sister and daughter at the same time, so she left the environment after a short while.

Her plan was to run away with me to my grandmother's place so she quietly sold few of her properties to buy tickets and enough food to last us throughout the journey. One night, while my grandfather and the children were sleeping outside the hut, - which was a custom for males, - she quietly got up, gathered our meager belongings and whatever clothes we had. Luckily, we didn't have much, thus it was easier for her to carry. She wrapped me in a small blanket and tried very hard to keep me from crying. As quickly as she could, she snuck into the dark of the night, silently walking just not to wake my grandfather up. Making it past my grandfather, she quietly walked out of the open gate in their fence made of branches and tree limbs. Without looking back, she slipped away into the night.

She walked quickly on the dark paths of Jawher while the village slept. Taking the trail through the countryside, she walked four miles to where the bus stopped every morning. She told me that she felt so relieved when we finally boarded the bus because she kept looking over her shoulder, fearing that her grandfather would come for us at any moment.

The bus ride to my grandmother's was about six hours on the main roads. We got off at a small town called Trejenta, in the middle of nowhere. Then she had to walk twenty-six miles – about 9 hours-through the bush and along small donkey-cart paths to get us to Balcad.

The journey was difficult for her. Though she was drenched in sweat, my mother was determined to reach the destination. Along the way, there were many wild animals, not to mention stray men lurking around to rob or rape as people passed by. She had to carry me, along with our belongings. Later in life, I walked that same path by myself many times. It was evident how a young girl or woman could get robbed or raped by camel boys. The path wound around farmer's fields, through heavy bush, around ponds and marshes and plateaus.

My grandmother was surprised to see us as she wasn't expecting us because there was no way to communicate with her beforehand – no mail or phone service in the bush of Somalia. We showed up at her hut late in the evening and my grandmother was very happy to see her only daughter with her new granddaughter. With great excitement, she told my mother she would slaughter a goat in the morning. We would have a feast to welcome visitors per our tradition; cooking it over the open fire and enjoying the feast with loved ones.

My mother's relief dissipated when she saw my grandfather who came unannounced on the eve of Ramadan at my grandmother's hut. "I want you back to my village immediately", he yelled at my mother. Both my mother and grandmother started to argue with him to let my mother stay. His response was, "You need to leave with me right now, the boys need you and I need you to raise them." He demanded that my mother returned with him to his village, or he would beat her up.

My mother refused to bring me back to his home and insisted   to stay with me at my grandmother's hut. My grandfather said, "You are my daughter, and you're coming with me."

She pleaded, "What will I do with my baby?" She pleaded as she looked at me and started crying. His only answer was, "I don't care. You are my daughter and you're coming with me. Period. I don't want to hear anything else!"

Overpowered, overwhelmed and saddened, my grandmother, bless her soul, told my mother, "Don't worry, I will take care of her." She offered to keep me with her and raise me as her own child. She knew that it would not be good for me to be brought back to live with my grandfather, where malaria and cholera were even more prominent than in grandma's village. My mother, with her heart pounding, her emotions torn apart looked at me one more time; tears of pain, anger, frustration, powerlessness ran down her cheeks. She reluctantly agreed to follow her father because disobedience was not part of the vocabulary. I can't imagine how difficult this might have been for her to make that   decision. As a mother, I cannot fathom what I would do if I were in her shoes.

My mother and I have spoken many times about this turn of events in our lives. I cannot blame her for leaving me with my grandmother. My mother did what she had to do to make it in a world which was not pleasant for a young teen mother. Being a teen mother myself, I do not know if I could do the same thing. I cannot imagine not seeing any of my children for more than few days or maybe a week. If I were not with them I would call and speak to them daily because I feel empty without them. My journey, growing up without my mother and father made me a better mother. I seek guidance about parenting always by reading the latest books about parenting to learn how to fill my children with joy, love, appreciation, and kindness. There is nothing better than lie on the floor with my son playing cards or reading a book. I watch him lying there, filled with happiness, smiling from ear to ear, and unable to contain his giggles. My child is very inquisitive, he asks questions more than a reporter. He always says "Mom this, mom that. Mom, why?" and I just roll with it because I know this will not last forever. He will soon grow and become his own man. I had him write a letter and sign it, stating he will always give me a hug, even in public after he hits puberty.

"Never wish life were easier, wish that you were better". - *Jim Rohn*
"It doesn't matter where you are coming from. All that matters is where you are going." - *Brian Tracy*

"As my mind can conceive of more good, the barriers and blocks dissolve. My life becomes full of little miracles popping up out of the blue." - Louise Hay

Chapter 2

FORGET KINDERGARTEN

"When life knocks you down, try to land on your back. Because if you can look up, you can get up. Let your reason get you back up." - Les Brown

---

Growing up in a small village out in the bush of Somalia is nothing like you would imagine unless you have experienced it yourself. If you've watched programs about village life in Africa showing huts built with sticks and branches, covered with rugs made of woven grass, naked babies and children running around, goats, sheep, cows with big horns, crocodiles in the river - then this would give you an idea of how I was raised.

Grandmother had a large herd of sheep, goats, and cows, so our milk was always fresh. We had no refrigerator, of course, because there was no electricity in the village, or anywhere for that matter. This meant we had to drink the milk throughout the day or it would spoil. Babies in the village were not given solid food until they turn two years old. Malnourishment is usually an issue. It was common to see babies with big stomachs due to lack of proper nutrition. The villagers weren't aware that babies need solid food by the time they're one. Their lack of education and understanding is not their fault, and there is a definite need to teach them about nutrition, cleanliness, and healthy living.

There wasn't a lot of affection going back and forth in village life. The villagers are country farmers, living off the land, grazing their animals, and working hard to survive every day in a very rugged environment. Compliments and recognition were nowhere to be found. Parents expected their kids to be task oriented. Grandmother was a tough woman, a shepherd, a farmer. She was strong worked hard all the time. She had a kind heart.

Like all toddlers in the village, I spent most of my time in the hut or outside within the confines of our fence in "hero." I had no siblings or friends to play with, so I would play in the dirt, bury myself, make little huts of my own. I would make baby dolls with parents out of sticks and twine, pretending that someday I would have a family of my own to care for. I even made breasts out of goat dung on the mother doll, and then wrapped a piece of cloth around them. I would make hair out of a certain tree branch that, when chewed, would become soft looking like hair. I'd have them wear a "maro" or wrap and, if married, they'd wear a covering on their head. If not, then they could show off their hair. I'd use water out and pretend it was food or meals. I'd use rocks as goats, cows and little babies. I'd make little fences to keep the animals in.

Nowadays, when I tell my daughters about how I used to play with the toys I'd make, they laugh at me and say that it's silly and gross. It was a lot different than their Barbie, tinker bell dolls and the play houses sold online or at the store.

My play spot was next to the hut in the dirt, which was sandy, much like playing in a sandbox. I also played under the tree where my uncles usually slept I always played by myself because the neighbors didn't have any kids my age and my uncles were too busy or not interested in playing with me. I was always warned not to wander outside the fence so I ended up spending a lot of time by myself. This prepared me for the long hours of loneliness when I had to take the animals out to graze. I quickly learned how to enjoy my own company. To this day, I have a hard time being fully social. I'm kind of a loner. Truthfully, I like spending time with me!

I found many ways to occupy my day. I would play with the animals inside their fences and spend time with the baby goats and sheep. They were so cute and I loved playing with them. I would try to milk them, but of course, they had no milk. I'd wander in with the cows to pet them, but some didn't like that, and they'd turn around and butt me. One time a cow threw me up in the air and after that experience, I stayed away from the cows. Those animals can easily step on when you get in the pen with them.

A young man, about fifteen years old, would walk past our "hero" – every day. He always went to "Dugsi", where the young men go for religious teachings and read the Quran. He saw me many times as he walked by and noticed that I was home alone. When Dugsi was over, rather than going back to his hut, he would come to ours. This was when the trouble began. He was mean and violent. Sometimes he would hit me with a stick, and then, abuse me sexually. This happened quite often. I hated when my grandmother and uncles would leave in the morning, as I knew this young man would come by.

He forbade me to inform my grandmother otherwise he would beat me horribly. I have kept it to myself to this day. At a young age, I learnt to tell myself that "it would be over soon, just bear with it." There was nothing I could do to stop him. He had control over me. One time, my legs were so marked up from him hitting me with a stick; I had to keep my dress down to my ankles so that my grandmother wouldn't notice the wounds.

I was very afraid of the consequences of my grandmother finding out about the ordeal. I was afraid that she would beat me with a stick, as she often threatened, even though it was in no way my fault. The young man knew that I had this fear, so he fueled it by saying how bad it would be if I told her. He told me what more he would do to me if my grandmother found out. This is how domination and abuse happen, through fear.

In the villages, there are no laws against child abuse - physical, emotional, or sexual. Everyone just agrees that it doesn't happen and ignores it. When it happens, you tell no one. One day, my grandmother and I came upon a woman being raped. Grandma told me, "Just turn the other way and keep walking." So, we did.

Looking back, it makes me mad at everyone: my grandmother, my uncles, my mother, everyone! Wouldn't it be better to be with my mother? There I was, left alone, vulnerable and being people's prey. Where was she and why wasn't she with me? Didn't I at least mean so much to any of them? Didn't my mother know what would happen to me?

I received the brunt of Grandmother's punishments growing up. When I was eight, we had an especially dry season. Everything was parched and dead, and we had to take the animals out far to graze them. It was a several days of walk. There was no green grass to feed the animals in our area. We had a cousin who was about ten years old. He came with us and brought his family's goats and sheep. My cousin and I would take the entire herd, his and ours, out grazing each day from our makeshift camp. My grandmother and Uncle Ahmed took the cows. This was my first experience as a nomad; staying out in the grasslands for months until the rainy season.

One evening, after my cousin and I brought the herd home, my grandmother asked us to go find wood so she could make fire and cook porridge for supper. We ventured away from the camp and ended up getting sidetracked by looking at the gorgeous birds and monkeys. Who wouldn't get sidetracked by monkeys? We lost track of time. We finally realized we had been gone too long, so we gathered up the sticks and branches and ran back to the camp. My grandmother was waiting. Anger can be clearly noticed in her countenance. She grabbed her walking stick with one hand and grabbed my arm with the other.

"What were you doing with your cousin out in the woods and why did it take you so long to get back?" I could barely open my mouth to answer when she started scolding me. I didn't know what to say so I just told her we were watching the monkeys. My cousin just stood still and watched; what else could he do? I had many bruises the following day.

Growing up, I wanted to please my grandmother and so I did everything to make her proud. I would take the cows out further; I would wash and groom them more often. I'd stay out all day grazing them, refusing to return home. I fought off jackals and hyenas for fear of losing a sheep or goat. I would wake up early to make tea for her. Through it all, I never heard her say, "Good job, Habibo." She never appreciated anything.

The lack of acknowledgment, appreciation, and acceptance, allowed me to go into overdrive with success when I came to America. I wanted to show everyone what I am made of. I wanted to show them that my years of training as a shepherd and a nomad weren't for nothing. The harsh environment allowed me to be more resilient and determined. It equipped me with the ability to bounce back quickly. Although I have pain, struggles, and self-doubt, I do not let those attributes stop me.

When I first came to America, I tried hard to forget my past: the shame, the feelings of worthlessness, and anger that came with it. I became busy with surviving and making a life for myself in this land of opportunity and I was successful at it. Several years later, when my daughter turned five years old, the same age I was molested, all the memories came crashing down on me.

A male cousin was visiting us for few days. One night, I had a nightmare. I dreamt that this cousin raped my daughter. In my dream, I was standing right in front of his face, holding a knife yelling, "I will kill you! You will not live if you did this to my daughter." Suddenly, I jumped out of bed and open my eyes. I was sweating; my nightgown, sheets, and pillow were drenched. I couldn't breathe. I was crying and trying to scream, but nothing was coming out of my mouth.

That was the beginning of my PTSD (post-traumatic stress disorder). Almost every night, I woke up out of the same nightmares. And I could vividly remember what had been done to me. I would fight in my dream and wake up gasping for air. I became completely consumed by the traumatic experiences from my past. I did not know what to do. I didn't have anyone to talk to and I didn't have the resources to help me work through the issues. I tried to go on with life as usual, pretending that nothing happened. It was like putting some items under your bed and pretending that they have never existed. But my emotions and the pain were eating me alive. Sometimes I would take my girls to the park and would be consumed with anxiety. I would think to myself, "Am I crazy? Can people see that my heart and my mind are racing?" I would get paranoid. I thought to myself, "What would happen to my girls if I go crazy right now and could not remember who I am and who they are?"

There were times I could not breathe and I would isolate myself from the rest of the mothers at the park because I did not want them to suspect something was wrong with me.

"Your thoughts and beliefs of the past have created this moment, and all the moments up to this moment. What you are now choosing to believe and think and say will create the next moment and the next day and the next month and the next year." - Louise Hay

I did not want to mention my feelings to anyone. I could smell a rat; I knew that something was wrong. The significant stigma shrouding mental health issue prevented many Somalis, including myself, from seeking treatment at that time, although I am no longer afraid of the stigma. In Somali culture, the concept of mental health is 'either crazy or not crazy'. There is no in-between. We believe that mental illness comes from God or evil spirits (jin). Mental Illness can also be brought on by another person or one's self through curses or bad behavior.

"You are not a helpless victim of your own thoughts, but rather a master of your own mind." - Louise Hay

Now that I am older and away from the village, I have had the necessary help that allowed me to sort through my feelings. I have found forgiveness. My Grandmother, with no education whatsoever, did the best she could, with what she had. Anger and pain used to be my fuel. These feelings pushed me to do better than anyone. What fuels me now is my kids and providing a good life for them. Through my children, I want to show the world the meaning of being loved and cared for. I want to show the benefits of being proud and confident in oneself that you have someone to confide in without fear of repercussion.

I want to be a part of something that helps change society, something greater than just my kids and I. If I can give back, I will. The universe has a plan for me. It shows me through my faith that there is something guiding me to make the right decision. I can sense it in the quieter moments. Today, I feel content heading where I need to be.

When I look at my son, exploring the world around him, my heart melts with happiness and gratitude. I am able to be fully present in his life. I am able to teach him and prepare him for the life ahead. He knows so much more than I did when I was eight years old. I am thankful he does not have to grow up the way I did. More importantly, he doesn't have to wonder whether he is loved or not because I tell him every chance I get and make a point to show him through my actions.

Chapter 3

TRAINED AS A SHEPHERD

My grandmother had seventy-five cows, forty-five goats, and ninety-five sheep. As soon as I could keep up, she started taking me out with her to learn how to herd the sheep and goats. My uncle, Ahmed, oversaw taking the cows out while my other uncle, Abdi, stayed at the farm with his wife to watch the young calves, sheep and goats. Abdi had a lot of physical ailments, one of them being untreated tuberculosis, so he stayed back tending to the young animals and taking care of the home site. My youngest uncle, Ali, attended full-time Dugsi at that time. He left for Mogadishu when I was 7 years old and I didn't see him again until many years later.

Grandmother Halima taught me all the paths to take through the grasslands. She taught me the daily routine of leaving the village the same way for two miles, navigating through the cropland, keeping the animals out of the farmers' fields, and finally out to the open grasslands and wooded areas. She carried her stick and, of course, I had mine. She was very patient, teaching me all the various whistles and sounds used to direct and call the herd. She carried a little bell with her, and when she rang it, all the sheep and goats would come running towards her. She mostly used it if we were in a wooded area to keep the herd together. If she needed their attention, she would ring it like she did when taking them to the river or bringing them home at night.

At midday, when the sun was beaming, we would take the herd back to the river to drink and rest. These are times I fondly remember. We would sit by the river, watching the animals; sometimes we would talk, sometimes we would not. Many times, I would lie in her lap and fall asleep. After an hour of rest, we would walk the animals out to the grasslands for the rest of the day and finally we headed home at sundown.

My grandmother was not always talkative when we would stop and rest; I was afraid of her, or you could say I respected her. I was just uncomfortable in her presence. Perhaps she had to be tough because she was living on her own. I was edgy about my performance and worried about getting punished if I did poorly. I loved her very much, and though she loved me as well, she never hesitated to give me a correction or a swat on the bottom with a stick. I have good memories of lying on her shoulder and cuddling when going to bed. When we were out in the grasslands with the animals, I had to be more focused, because the sheep and goats were our livelihoods; without them, we would starve. Even at the early age of four or five, I had difficulty relaxing. I often felt anxious and tensed compared to girls of my age.

One of the times we went out to the grasslands, we had two sheep ready to give birth. Grandmother helped the first sheep have its baby as I watched. She explained everything to me; showed me how to help the baby come out, making sure it was turned the right way, while comforting the mother. After it was born, she said, "Ok, Habibo, the next one you can help. Since you're going to be taking care of them, you'll need to know how to do it."

When the sheep's water broke, I first rubbed the liquid around the sheep's bottom to relax it; this allowed it to be more flexible and stretch for the baby lamb to come out. Usually, the feet come first. I took hold of the feet, they were wet and hard to hold onto, and then I gently rotated the lamb out.

Few years later, I had a difficult time birthing a baby goat. I was out herding with two girls I came across on the way and suddenly one of the goats went into labor. Of course, I was way out in the grasslands, several miles from the village. One foot came out, but the other didn't. The goat was struggling and couldn't walk anymore. I could not leave this pregnant goat alone. I had to stay with her and help if necessary. The two girls I was with that day said, "Just leave it, who cares?

"No, I'll be in big trouble and get whipped if I lose a goat." I responded.

I was more worried that the poor mother would be eaten alive by hyenas during the night. The girls decided to leave me out there in the grasslands by myself, while they took the herds back home. I was crying and I didn't know what to do. I was certain to get in trouble if I lost a sheep. I got on my knees and prayed to God that somehow, I would be saved from this situation. It was getting dark and I was so afraid to be out there by myself. Finally, a man, walking towards the village, came by; he was older and very nice. He offered to carry the goat back to the village. I was so grateful for his help. The goat lived and the baby was born with the help of my grandmother.

One day my uncle Abdi and I took the herds out further than my grandmother and I ever went. He showed me the way to take the animals through the grasslands as far as Mount Bordeer. And he said, "Habibo, this is as far as you can go." The day was cut short because it was Ramadan, and my uncle had to fast, meaning no food or water. Foolishly, I forgot to bring water with me, and there was none in sight, as it was the dry season. We walked, for what seemed like forever, until midday when the sun was right above our heads. I was dying of thirsty and said, "Uncle, I am thirsty." He answered, "I am sorry, there is no water." We were in a vast open land where no one lived. Feeling my pain, Abdi finally said, "OK, you can go back. I'll keep on going."

I started walking back home. I remembered the sun shining on my face. It was very hot that day, 115 degrees or more. I was wearing sandals made from old tires. When it's hot out, these sandals get extremely hot as if you are walking on fire. They were the cheapest of all shoes; most girls didn't wear them. Since I didn't have anyone to say, "No, she is a girl and needs better shoes," that's what I wore.

Walking back through the dry, dusty grasslands, I kept seeing mirages of water in the distance. I thought, "Oh, water!", as my throat got drier, my tongue stuck out and my lips twitched. I kept walking, eventually making it out of the bush area into a dry, empty land. The mirages became one vision after another. It was stark with no vegetation, and the ground was hard as a rock. I walked for several miles. Since it was the dry season, I couldn't even find fruit to eat for moisture. I kept walking, thinking, "I am getting close! I am getting close!" Yet, no water.

I finally couldn't walk anymore, because my feet were burning tremendously. I took my shoes off because I was getting blisters all over my feet. I finally walked barefoot. The last thing I remembered was feeling very light headed, barely able to walk another step. I needed to sit down, but couldn't. I knew that, if I wanted to live, I needed to get to a water hole or get home, which was still at least ten miles away. I kept saying to myself, "You can do this. You got this, Habibo. You are not a quitter."

I must have passed out because I remembered waking up in a nomad's shelter. It was little more than some branches put together with a woven rug thrown over it to keep the sun out. When I gained consciousness, I was there with just the man because his wife was still out with their herd. He told me that he was on his way back from the city when he found me laying on the ground in the bright sunlight. I recognized him from when our paths crossed while herding the animals with my grandmother, so I wasn't scared. In addition, he was of the same tribe as my uncles.

"How did I get here?" I asked him

He responded, "I picked you up because you passed out in the desert all by yourself. When I got you home, I gave you cold water, you took a few sips, and I patted you with more water to cool you off. I waited until you woke up because I don't know where your hut is."

I remembered telling him how thirsty I was, so he gave me a big water jug. I finished it so fast that I started vomiting. His wife came home late in the day and gave me some milk to drink. "Slowly," she said. By this time, it was dark out. She asked me where I lived and I told her.

The man took me home. We got there about 9:00 or 10:00 at night. We found my grandmother and uncles sitting around the fire having dinner. They didn't know where I had been. They were worried, but not too worried that they would come out looking for me. Instead, they scolded me and said, "Why would you do that, Habibo, leaving your water jug at home?" They drilled me with questions. The man who found me said, "This child passed out in the desert, she was so thirsty, how could you leave a child out like that?" Abdi was eating his dinner and retorted, "Well, she didn't take water with her. She should have taken water."

That was a tough lesson for a seven-year-old girl. I can assure you that I never forgot to bring water on a trek like that again. I realize now that my uncle should have made sure we had water with us; young children are expected to grow up very fast when they live out in the country to survive. They also must be independent enough to herd the animals at a young age.

Shortly after, my grandmother and uncles decided I was ready to take the sheep and goats out by myself. First, they wanted me to spend time taking the herd out with our two neighbor girls, Sarah and Alma. They were about ten or eleven years old and had been herding their animals together since they were five. I was excited to be on my own with no one watching my slightest move and correcting me. I thought that I could play a little while the herd was grazing. Maybe I could play with the other girls in the dirt and make my own dolls out of sticks.

The first day we went out, I got up early around 4:30 a.m. I was nervous, but excited that I was going out with two older girls. I was excited to think we could be friends. I foresee their mean spirits towards me. After my morning chores were done, and the sun rising up, my grandmother made me porridge for breakfast. I filled my tiny bottle with water (something left over from when the Italians were in the country) and closed it. Grandma and I let the goats and sheep out of their pen and counted each one prior to our departure

I saw them coming down the lane that passed in front of our hero (fence). We let our herd out and they all mixed together. All together, we had about two hundred animals. It was an exciting way to start the day. Off we went, on our way out of the village into the wide-open grasslands. The herd started moving quickly. We took them through the paths that wound through farmers' croplands, making sure they didn't get into their fields. One of the girls was at the back of the herd, one on the side, with me on the opposite side. The fastest goat was leading the whole pack. Once we got past the crop land, we let them go.

We didn't bring any food with us, only water. If we were lucky, we might find some fruit out in the land or dig out some roots to eat; but we had nothing else to eat. I quickly learnt that the two girls were not going to be friends with me. Instead, they ended up bullying me.

In the grasslands, we would run into other young people with their herds. The girls would get together with their friends, talking and laughing. I ended up being their gopher; they had me do all the work, while they sat with their friends. They would say, "Habibo, go get that sheep. Habibo, run and get this, run and get that." The girls and their friends would pick on me; telling me that my clothes were not nice and that I was not pretty. They would make me do all the work for them, while the older girls would play with other teenage girls and boys.

I guess bullying occurs even in the dessert of Somalia. It was the longest few months of my life. Each day, by midday, we would take the herd out to the river. It was usually alright; except the girls would go swimming and I didn't know how to swim. So, I was left to watch the goats and sheep. I did my best to talk to the herd, to make them sit and rest for a while under the trees by the river. After an hour or so, we'd take the herd out into the grasslands before bringing them home at night.

One time, the girls wanted me to watch their herd while they went off to play. I said, "OK, I'll do that", but I just sat under a tree and ignored the herd. Most of the animals, especially the ones who had babies, always wanted to get back to the village. So, they left and went home. The girls were swimming and playing with the boys, having no idea that more than half the herd was heading back to the village. The girls came back and as we were counting the herd, we noticed that almost thirty animals went missing. They were upset, asking, "Where did they go? Where are they?" I acted stupid and told them I didn't know what happened. They started to panic; they told me to stay with the herd, while they went to search for the missing animals, but they couldn't find any of them. Their plan was to finish up and then go home. "We will tell our parents we don't know what happened", they said.

We got home by 3:00 in the afternoon, which was a big no-no; it's too early to stop grazing. I remembered the older girls being so worried getting into trouble. I got home and my grandmother asked, "What happened?" She was home and all her sheep and goats came walking in through the main gate. I said, "We were swimming and they escaped." For some reason, someone was smiling on me that day, because there was no punishment. That was a relief.

I continued with the girls for a few months, until I came to my senses and realized they were just mean and cruel. I preferred to go out on my own and not to mess with the girls and their herd. I learnt how to count the herd each day before I left home, and each night before I came back. The other children in the village had to do the same thing. Miraculously, all the animals knew which herd to stay with and which compound they belonged to. They would follow the lead goat and the shepherd, which was me. From that day on, until I left the village, I took the animals out, seven days a week, all year long for more than sixteen hours a day.

Grandmother taught me how to survive out in the wild. She taught me how to save my supply of water so it can last the whole day and how to make ropes out of a certain tough tree bark. She also taught me how to keep an eye out for other animals that would lurk and try to steal one of the herds. I learned how to listen to the sounds of different animals. I would hear them out in the bush without seeing them; hyenas and jackals, bush pigs and the African wild dog. Jackals would mainly be around during the day and hyenas loved to come out at night.

They always make a yipping sound. They were hard to see because they had a grayish brown color which was the same color as the grass. The jackals would find a way to sneak up on the herd and hide behind trees and rush out at the animals when you least expect it. The sheep would run in different directions as they have no sense of direction. The jackals would chase them all over and I would run as fast as I could, yelling at them, shaking my walking stick and chasing them away to make sure they didn't get any of my animals.

However, one time when I was about six years old and out on my own and I couldn't chase the jackals away. They killed a baby goat and strangled a sheep. I was sitting far away and playing with other kids from a different village, when I noticed my goats and sheep were running off in opposite directions, with several jackals running after them. We had a baby goat only a few months old, and I could see the jackals were going for it. I jumped up and ran as fast as I could, but the jackal grabbed it, and the poor little goat was twirling in the jackal's mouth. I was running, yelling and chasing it as it was running with the goat in its mouth. I was trying to make as much noise as possible. The jackal finally let go, dropped the baby goat and ran away, but I was too late. The little goat was laying in the grass, bleeding and having difficulty breathing. I sat by the dying baby goat, petting it, trying to soothe it and calming it down.

I had to chase after the other goats because they were still running aghast. Once the goats calmed down and stopped running, I came back to the baby goat on the ground and found out she was dead. There was nothing left for me to do, so I just walked away. I felt sick to my stomach and started shaking and vomiting. I was afraid I would get whipped for losing a goat, which I did. "Habibo, how could you not have your eyes open? How could you let that happen?" It was hard to take at only six years old.

It was one of those days when you should not leave the house. That same day, while watching the herd, I noticed the sheep were scattering. I ran toward them, trying to see what the problem was. A large jackal got a hold of a baby sheep and grabbed it on the side. There were two jackals after the sheep, so I threw my walking stick and hit one on the back. It ran off. The other jackal was running after another sheep, but once it noticed that its companion ran off, it did, too.

There's a saying in Somalia that hyenas and jackals understand: "If I knew which sheep belonged to a woman, I wouldn't touch it" meaning, a woman's possessions are not to be touched. If you do, you're doomed, because she'll never forget it. I think perhaps that's true in many situations with women in general, not just when it comes to sheep and goats!

I learnt a lot from my Grandma, about herding animals and life. By the time, I was seven, I was taking the herd of cows out, rather than the goats and sheep which Grandma took over. One of the most important things she taught me was how to be patient with the animals, especially the cows. They would fight or go off in different directions, so it was easy to get frustrated and upset. With cows, you can't do that. You must find a way to take care of the situation without making it worse. I talked to the cows, told them where we were going like, "Go to the river", "Go home", "Let's go this way." I also learned to sing to the cows in different ways to soothe them. Each one of the cows had names, so I could call them by name. When the cows were full from grazing, they would lie down and get comfortable. This was a nice time for me because the walking would end for a while and I could sit down with them specially Dinjar my favorite cow. I would lay on her, pat her and talk to her, sometimes falling asleep with her. Some cows would seek me out and wanted to be petted. If they had a bug, I would take it off. The cows were my friends and I trusted them more than the kids in the village.

One thing about animals is they cannot disappoint you. What's not to love about them? The cows made me feel like I was responsible. I would take them far away if it was dry; I'd graze them, find water, and feel a sense of accomplishment knowing I helped them make it through one more day. When I would bring them home, the people in the village would say, "Oh, Habibo, your cows are full. They look so good." It was my grandmother I was hoping to get a compliment or approval from, but she didn't.

One time, a younger girl from the village came along with me so she could learn how to be a shepherd. I was around seven and she was five. We would graze our herds together. We took the herd by the river to a nice spot where we could let the animals eat, play and lay by the river to rest. She and I had fun making little dolls out of sticks. We made them with grass for hair and dressed them in tree leaves.

When it was time to get going towards the end of the day, we counted the herd and realized we were missing one. We counted several times. It was one of mine that was missing. I started to panic. She counted hers and they were all there. I started running around calling the goat's name, but I couldn't find it. We went home knowing I was going to get punished. I explained to my Grandma that the goat with the missing horn was missing. I told her I didn't know what happened and I was watching the herd all day. Surprisingly, Grandma was fine with it and didn't punish me.

She just said, "Let's hope she doesn't get eaten by crocodiles. Did you count them before you took them to the river?"

I told her, "I am sure she was there when I took them to the river. Whatever happened occurred after we got to the river."

She told me, "You're supposed to be more alert; listening for distress sound, rather than playing."

Grandma, Ahmed and I went back to the river and trailed all the way through the woods. While calling the goat's name and whistling for her, we heard a noise near the river. We looked around and made our way over to the cliffs that line one side of the river. There, we saw the goat. She had fallen down the cliff and was hanging by a little snag, almost ready to fall into the river. To make it worse, it was an area known for crocodiles.

My uncle was so mad... I have never seen him that upset before.

"What is this now?" he cried, "How do I get that sheep out now? I must go into the river to get it out. I don't know what else to do."

We tried to make a rope, but not in time - the goat ended up falling into the river. My hands were shaking; I was crying and afraid I would piss on myself. I was worried the goat would be eaten by crocodiles. It was a wide river and very dangerous.

The water was turbulent, and the goat was pulled by the waves down the river. Ahmed and I ran along the bank of, watching her the whole time. The goat tried to swim, but kept being pushed farther into the river. My grandma couldn't keep up.

Suddenly, Ahmed jumped into the river ahead of the goat and grabbed her by the horns. He had to swim to get her out, as the water was deep and the current was flowing fast. This time, I didn't get a scolding. Ahmed and Grandma were mad at me and told me to never do that again. Luckily, I didn't get whipped – how on earth did I pull that off?

On another occasion, I took our goats and sheep to the river to drink. I was sitting back on the bank, watching the animals and talking with my neighbor. It was about midday; extremely hot and the animals were thirsty. They all lined up in a row at the edge of the river with their mouths down to the water while we were having a small chat on a grassy hill. Suddenly they all stopped drinking and lifted their heads; all in unison! It was odd to see, almost like it was choreographed. The whole herd, at the same time, started to walk backwards, looking straight ahead at the water.

Suddenly, we could see one of the younger sheep, bent over with its butt sticking out of the water. We stood up quickly, just in time to see a crocodile with the young sheep's head in its mouth. The crocodile quickly twirled around in the water with the sheep in its mouth and dove beneath the surface. When a crocodile peer above the water and pick out their meal, it does its best to get it and hones in on the prey. The most difficult part of herding them was when the bulls fought. I had to be able to break up their fights. We had three bulls while the rests were cows, totaling about fifty. All you could do was to go as far away as possible from them, or they'd kill you, charging at you if they were mad. I was afraid of them. Usually, if they were fighting, I would ignore them, but I had many close calls. The whole village had about ten bulls; they knew each other and wouldn't stop until one of them won. We had the cutest bull in the village so everyone wanted him to breed their cows.

The biggest mistake I ever made was attempting to break a fight when our favorite bull was involved. Another herd from the village was grazing close to mine, and their bull, a large one, started fighting ours. I felt sorry for him, getting beat up by this huge bull. My bull fell and the other one was butting it with its horns. I took my walking stick and hit the large bull on its side as hard as I could try to scare it off. The large bull turned around, snorted and pawed the ground. He charged with his head down and horns pointed directly at me. I ran like never before, got behind a tree and grabbed onto it. The tree was just enough to force him to back off. Meanwhile, my young bull had run away. I broke up the fight, but I could have been the one to lose in the end.

One day, I was herding the cows by myself, when I encountered two teenage boys. They wanted a farmer's crop, so they let their cows eat his barley.

After their herd stripped his field, the boys took their cows and left. I didn't know this was happening between the boys and the farmer. As I was walking my cow's home, I saw the farmer. He was furious and charged towards me. I knew him and thought, "He's one of the Tumalles." He came towards me with a long stick. He said, "How dare you let your cows eat my barley!"

"I don't know what you're talking about. I didn't do anything. My cows didn't do it." I responded

He hit me twice with his stick, and I took off. He ran after me and I fell he grabbed me, whipped me again and took my herd of cows to his home. I ran home crying and bleeding. My uncle, Ahmed, was surprised to see me, "What's going on? What's happening?" He inquired

I told him about the farmer. He asked, "He hit you?" He was furious. He went after the farmer, "how dare you beat my niece. She is such a young girl?"

"I'm sorry. I found out it wasn't your cows who ate my crops; I shouldn't have done that. I so was angry. Someone else told me it was not your cows. I am sorry"

Uncle Ahmed scolded him, and the farmer offered a goat as an apology. Ahmed left him off.

I had many experiences in Somalia that would seem strange or scary to people living in the western world but to us, it was part of daily living. Many incidents occurred by the river, as it was a focal point for the village, as well as wild animals.

The crocodiles were nothing to mess with. Occasionally, they'd come up to the shore and eat a goat or baby goat drinking by the side of the river. Sometimes, the crocodiles would kill people. When a crocodile was spotted, everyone would call the young men in the village. They would try to capture and kill it before it killed someone. Many times, I saw the men trying to catch a crocodile, splashing in the water, throwing a rope around it. It was quite a sight.

I did witness a young girl devoured by a huge crocodile. We were down by the river, swimming and enjoying the cool water, when suddenly, there was a big splash. We all looked over at the sound to notice a monster crocodile grab one of the younger girls by her head. She was flailing and kicking. It twisted around quickly, its tail powering it around. It pulled her into the water. It happened so fast. We started screaming and trying to help her; swimming towards her to grab her legs as she was kicking, but it was too late. The crocodile dove under the water with the girl in its mouth, and that was the last we saw of her.

Later that day, the young men captured the crocodile that ate the young girl; they killed it, dragged it out of the water and cut it in half, but the girl wasn't in there. She was probably left under the bank of the river or in some weedy area. Crocodiles take their prey and hide it in the river, then eat it later.

Chapter 4

SURVIVING MALARIA

According to the World health organization report, "a child dies every minute from malaria in Africa, where it is estimated that 9 out of 10 malaria deaths occur. In 2013, there were 528,000 deaths from malaria and about 78% of these were children under 5 years of age. Malaria is transmitted via the bites of infective mosquitoes, but unknown to many; it can also be spread to children during pregnancy as well as before and/or during childbirth."

I had malaria more than a dozen times in my life and survived it. Growing up out in the bush country, getting malaria was the same as getting the common cold here in the USA. It was a household term, and each year it would take its toll on the African population. The World Health Organization has labeled it as the main child killer on the continent. In the villages and out in the country, all the standing water and ponds during the two rainy seasons breed mosquitoes which cause an epidemic of malaria. We always considered ourselves lucky if we do not catch malaria and always hope we get luckier the next season too.

Whenever we had malaria, we would let it run its course because there was no access to medication or vaccinations outside the main cities. We couldn't prevent it or fight it. We hoped for the best that we could beat the bouts of fever. We had no screens over the doors to our huts, no mosquito mesh over where we slept.

Sadly, I saw many die from malaria in our village. It's a terrible disease. The shaking chills are when your fever gets so high; first, you go out of your mind, and secondly, you burst into sweat and chills, day after day. Many times, I have seen bodies of relatives and friends taken outside the village to an area designated for burial. Here, there were no headstones, footstones or even names to mark their graves.

One of the worst bouts happened to me in 1989 when I was about seven. It was the rainy season and mosquitoes flock the area – down by the river, in the ponds, out in the grasslands, even in our own cow yard. I got bitten and within few days I was sick. With malaria, your fever runs high and you become very chilled with extremely strong shakes. It seems like the trademark of malaria is the shaking chills and fever that brings you right out of your head. My fever reached at least 106 degrees. It would then spike and drop and spike again. Dehydration sets in quickly, and soon I couldn't walk because I was so weak.

I spent my days lying in the hut on a mat covering my wooden bed. I was covered with a thin blanket because I had the shaking chills from fever. Sometimes, to get into the warm air, I would lie under the big tree where my uncle, Ahmed slept. I couldn't eat or drink much. My fever ran very high. Most of the time, I was in a state of delirium. My grandmother once sent my uncle, Abdi, to Beledwayne to purchase some medications for malaria, but even that did not cure my illness. Many times, the medications in Somalia are expired and would not do anything for you.

About a month later, it had not rained in our village, so my grandmother and Ahmed decided that we had to move our animals out into the grasslands to graze them for a few months. This meant living as nomads to keep the animals alive, like we had done several times before. They decided to take me along with them, with the hopes that I'd get better and could help herd the animals.

They got all the animals ready to go. They gathered the belongings needed for survival, and packed them onto the donkey cart, as I laid sick in the hut or under the tree. One of the benefits of being sick was I didn't have to do anything. Early the next morning, they loaded me on top of the big pile of belongings we were taking along. They had packed pots, pans, food, water jugs, utensils, branches and rugs to build a hut, and a few other essentials. The clothes we brought were the clothes we had on our backs! I rode on a little makeshift bed with a blanket as we made our way through the dry and dusty grasslands, formerly verdant with green growth. We slowly walked, perhaps twenty-five miles a day, to get to the grassy areas that were still having rain. We had about forty cows, seventy-five sheep and goats, and three donkeys which took turns pulling the cart with me on top. Grandmother walked up front leading the herd, while Ahmed handled the donkey cart from behind.

We left the village and walked about half a day. We rested for the night, throwing together a makeshift hut with few branches and rugs thrown over them. Grandma would cook a little porridge, but my stomach could not contain any food. I just laid in the hut and shivered. We traveled again the next day for half a day, rested half a day, and continued this way for several days.

I remembered being so glad I was sick because that meant I didn't have to walk. The walk kills you; your feet hurt so bad, you're exhausted and hot and you can't stop. It's not just the walking. It's keeping the animals in place, too, so you don't lose any of them. If one of them were not able to walk, you help them. If one got lazy and sat down, you must get it up moving. If one tried to run away, you would run after it with your walking stick and bring it back. You get so tired, that you can hardly walk anymore. You're constantly walking and in a state of hunger.

I spent most of the time in a state of delirium, hallucinating. My grandmother was worried about me because it was the sickest she had ever seen me. She told me, years later, that I would wake up in the middle of the night and walk around; hallucinating and talking nonsense because of my high fever. I felt bad that she had to worry about me, as well as the animals. I don't remember many of the experiences.

The donkey and cart forced us to travel using the paths that meandered through open grasslands made by other nomads before us. After the third day of walking, suddenly it started getting greener. The animals began their grazing as they were hungry from the walk without having much food.

Grandmother and Ahmed found an abandoned camp used by other nomads. They decided to stop there and camp. It was a good spot, out in the open where they could watch the herd. There was already a makeshift frame for a hut, a corral with branches and brush to keep the animals in at night. It is very common for nomads to use and leave those sites. You'd never find any utensils or anything useful left behind as they were too precious.

Ahmed would take the cows and Grandma the goats and sheep. They would head out to graze each day at sunrise and return just sundown. I would lay there by myself with some water to drink and a little porridge. That was my breakfast, lunch and dinner if I could eat anything at all. I would just lie there shivering and shaking, hallucinating, not even sure where I was. If I could, I'd step outside the hut. I would lie in the hot sun under my blanket. The sun made me feel better because I was always chilled, and my teeth were rattling. Also, being out in the sun is one of the ways to kill the malaria bacteria. Over a three-month period, I got so sick that I lost about twenty pounds. I could barely eat and drink. Sometimes my grandmother would soak tobacco and give me the juice to drink. It was so bitter and had a disgusting taste. I was so high after that I am certain I could dance on any reggae music. It made me feel better and I was able to walk around for a while. But it did not cure my ailment. After the effect of the tobacco in my system, I felt even sicker.

One of the most common home remedies our village used to cure malaria was to wash the sick person with warm animal blood and leave it on for twenty-four hours. I had to endure this several times, as I had malaria so many times in my life. The smell of the blood was unbearable to me. The sight of blood irks my stomach. I probably don't need to tell you that this does not work; it's folk medicine. It was believed to help for some reason. I can't tell.

After a while the animals grazed in that green pasture as much as they could from that area and like nomads do, we had to move and find more grazing zones for them.

Off we went again looking for better grasslands. My health did not improve. On the contrary I felt sicker and sicker. At the same moment, my cousin, Farhiyo, who was about seven and living in our village, also caught malaria. She passed away from the disease.

We traveled from the camp, up in the mountains to a new site near a small village where the grass was green. My grandmother was resource less, worried to lose me. She decided to   contact   my mother and see if she could take me to Mogadishu to get the necessary medical help. My grandmother went to the little village near us where she found a man who was indeed traveling to the capital and she directed him to my grandfather's house where my mother resided. The man found my mother and gave her the message. I owe my life to that man. Had he somehow failed to find my mother, I would not be telling this story today.

It was late in the afternoon, around 5 o'clock, I was lying under a tree by myself, covered with a small blanket when I suddenly saw my mother emerging from the bushes I thought I was hallucinating, as I hadn't seen her in several years. It was her, my mother. I was so excited to see her; I cried with joy. I wanted to get up and run toward her give her a hug but my weak legs could not respond. I collapsed on the ground. She reached out to hold and hugged. I could feel her heartbeat and the warmth of her body. I felt reassured.

She sat me down and took care of me. She gave me water to drink and carried me into the hut, and cleaned me off from all my sweat.

My mother slept next to me in the hut the whole night. The following day, we left early to catch the bus. We had to make the journey through the bush to the main road and she carried me on her back, with my legs around her waist and my arms around her neck. We were fortunate to catch a ride with someone who was going half way in our direction. We rode on his donkey cart. Then she walked for fifteen miles to go carrying me on her back. Oh mother, you are an awesome woman! Periodically, she had to sit down and rest. My mother is a small woman, about 5'2", but strong. She was about twenty-four years old at the time. Once we arrived at the bus station, we waited hours for the bus to arrive. I laid on the ground with my blanket, and my mother bought tea with milk to drink because I was not able to eat solid food.

Finally, the bus arrived and we boarded. This was my first time being in a motorized vehicle. As soon as the bus drove away, I began to get car sick. I could not hold it anymore; I just had to let it out. I vomited on my mother and the lady sitting across from us.

My mother said, "Habibo! Why didn't you tell me you were going to vomit? I could have given you a bag!"

"I am afraid." I responded

"I'm your mother and you should not be afraid of me." She said in a reassuring tone. I felt relieved because I was not scolded.

On the way, I was in and out of consciousness. After six hours of ride we finally reached Mogadishu. We got off the bus and took a taxi to my mother's apartment. When we got out of the taxi, I could not believe what I was seeing. It was the biggest and tallest building I had ever seen. It was at least eight stories tall. My mother lived on the fifth floor, in an apartment that had three bedrooms and one bathroom. When we got there, she gave me a shower. I had never taken a shower before. I had always washed in the river or ponds near the village. I was so exhausted that I could not eat. I just wanted to lie down. She took me to a beautiful room with a big bed, a thick blanket, and sheets, which I had never laid on before. Oh, and a pillow. This was the first time I had ever seen these things, and it was so exciting to me. I felt like I had gone to live in a queen's palace. My mother lived there with her husband and no kids. Right then, I decided I was going to stay there with her. I would not return to my grandma's village. There was plenty of room for me here. This made me grateful that I was so sick. I had never been in such a nice place in all my life.

The next day, we went to the hospital and the doctors found out that I indeed had malaria, as well as a parasitic infection in my stomach. I was also severely anemic. They put me on four different medications and I received injections in my hips twice a day for three weeks. The doctor sent me back home, but I had to return to the hospital each morning and afternoon, every day for three weeks, to receive more injections. They were big needles! It's was a bit traumatizing. In addition, I had to be on oral medications. My mother could not get me to swallow the large pills because they were so bitter. All the injections I had to receive caused my hips to became swollen and blown up like a soft ball. One of the injection sites on my right hip got infected. My mom had to ice it a few times each day. Unfortunately, it created sciatic nerve problems in my right hip. I don't think they even knew what a sciatic nerve was in that hospital.

Two weeks later, I began to feel better. Each day, I would sit on my mother's balcony and gaze through the railing to watch the kids playing down on the dirt street. They would play soccer for hours. I couldn't believe that they were doing nothing with their time but playing for hours, with no chores or anything else to do. I thought to myself, "How could those kids have free time like that?" I thought about how lucky they were. I asked my mother if I could go play with them, but she said that I was still too sick to go play outside and advised me to watch them from the balcony.

After I completed my treatment, my mother allowed me to go play with the kids. We played stuff I didn't even know how to play. They didn't like me because city kids and country kids don't mix well together. They could tell by how I spoke that I was from the country. Their language was a little more refined – I thought-, whereas mine was cruder.

Sometimes, my mother would let me go grocery shopping for her. One time, she took me shopping for a new "ambuuer", a long dress, and sandals. I asked her, "What are those for? I have lots of clothes already." I thought it was extravagant because when I lived with grandmother in the village, all I had was one dress.

My mom told me we were going to visit my dad the next day. "Oh really, say walahi; you're not joking about this?" I jumped up with excitement.

And she said, "Yes, it is the truth. You will meet your father tomorrow"

I was so happy that I was going to see my father, I was sleepless and restless. I tossed and turned all night. I couldn't wait until the next morning. I wanted to be ready and out of the door early. I woke my mom up at 7 o'clock in the morning, thinking that we were going to leave soon. My mom told me that we would be going in the afternoon. She said we never visit anyone in the morning. By 3 o'clock in the afternoon, people in Somalia are done with their daily business and stay home for the rest of the day. I waited until two o'clock.

Finally, mom and I left. We walked for half a mile to get to the bus station. We boarded the bus, which took about 30 minutes to the destination. The house was blue with a brown gate at the entrance. My father and his second wife lived there with their four children. As we entered the compound, one of my little sisters ran up to us, asking who we were. My stepmother, my two other sisters and my brother came out to greet us. After a few minutes, my mother left me and said that she would be back in two days. I was so happy to be at my dad's house.

As the evening wore on, I asked my step mother several times when my dad was going to come home. She told me not to wait up because he was not coming anytime soon. My dad did not get home until we were all asleep. When I woke up the next morning, I went to my dad's room to find that he has left for the day. I was so sad, I cried in the bathroom. The whole day felt like years; all I wanted was to see my father. The next morning, I woke up very early and walked into his room. I saw him sleeping. I ran up to his bed to say hello to him. He gave me a hug and told me that I had grown. He said that it was good to see me. He had to go back to sleep, so I came out and went back to sleep. That was my last encounter with my father. My expectations, excitement and joy were met with emptiness, just a tap on the back from my father. I was sad and I am still sad. All I wanted to do was build a connection with him. I wanted to create that bond between us. I wanted to know that he cared. I wanted to know that he thought of me and after all I was his first born. But to my disappointment there was none of those things. There has always been a hole in my heart because all I ever wanted was to be with my dad or be daddy's little girl for once. I can remember that experience as if it were yesterday. Why our interaction was so short? Don't I deserve to be in his presence? Am I not good enough? Am I not worthy of his presence?

Three days later, my mother came and took me back to her house. I felt pain and unwanted. I wanted to stay with my father and I wanted to be a part of his family. I was missing that and I was deprived of that. Deep down I know that would be the last time I would see my father. I knew that whatever hope I had died there that day when I left. A lot of my sadness and anger come from my father's absence in my life. I longed for a relationship with him. I have always felt like the outcast on my father's side of the family. A child needs his or her parents' affection and affirmation. For a daughter getting love from her dad is enormously immeasurable. How he treats her sets the tone for so many other relationships in her life. Every boy or man she meets will automatically be measured against her dad, and that relationship. He is her ultimate standard and role model for manhood. Without him, how am I supposed to know how a man should treat me. When two people get divorced, there are still responsible for their child. I wished many times that my father would walk into our 'hero', bring me presents and take me away from the harsh life. It never happened. It broke my heart and still does in many ways. Sometimes I wonder whether and how things would have been different for me, had I grown up with my father. It leaves my heart empty in many ways, even now that I am in my thirties. Part of me is still that little girl who longed to be with her dad; the little girl who searched for his affection and words of affirmation. Sometimes, I cry because I yearn to be in his presence; I want to feel his touch and be in his arms, even for a moment. I have difficulty trusting men and for so long I did not know why. Later, I understood that my issues are from my father's absence in my life.

One day, my mother told me that I needed to go back to the village. No way! Back to the nomad life again? Why? Why me? My heart sank. I was having so much fun; more fun than I have ever had. I felt so happy to have friends to play with. Living with my mother felt so wonderful. I pretended to be sick again because I didn't want to go back. I was so scared to voice my refusal to go back to the nomad life. I wanted to be with my mother. I did not want to go back to the harsh environment with my grandmother in the village. She told me I was ready to go back. I felt nauseous. I couldn't understand why I couldn't stay with her, especially because she had so much room and seemed to have enough money to take care of me. I thought about the other children playing outside. I wished so badly to be like one of them; living with my parents, having friends, and going to school. I knew the harsh life I was going to face in the village – work and criticism every day, with no affection.

"If I am going, I want to take a present to my grandmother." I told my mother. I knew there was only one thing that would make my grandmother happy – sugar! She liked it more than gold. My mother bought ten pounds of sugar and a few bags of black tea. My mother also helped me buy a bottle of sesame oil, a pair of shoes for my uncle Ahmed, and a dress for my grandmother.

I expected my mother to come with me to the village. Instead, she brought me to the bus station in Mogadishu early one morning, said goodbye and put me on the bus. I was so nervous. I pleaded with her to come with me, but she said she couldn't. I was so fearful. I was worried I would throw up on the bus like I did before. I wondered why I couldn't stay.

Wasn't I good enough? Didn't she love me or want me? I felt rejected.

I reluctantly boarded the bus and sat next to a lady going in the same direction. She asked why I was traveling alone. I explained that I was going back to my grandmother's village, Balcad, and my mother couldn't come. She was surprised that I was traveling alone. She was so kind, giving me some fruits, which I ate sparingly, for fear of throwing up. She comforted me.

The bus got to Trejenta, about seventeen miles from Balcad, in the early evening. Both the lady and I got off the bus; she was heading south and I had to go north. I had way too much to carry – ten pounds of sugar, packages with shoes and a dress, a bottle of oil, tea, along with the items my mother bought for me. The lady I traveled with said, "Why did you bring all this?" I said, "My grandma likes tea, so when I get home I can make tea with sugar for her." It was all too heavy to carry alone. The lady spoke to the shopkeeper at the bus stop and asked if I could leave some of my items there. He accepted. I carried the sugar and tea bag with me. The lady told me to take care of myself, to be careful walking home and then she went on her way. There I was, left alone, seven years old, at a bus stop in the middle of the Somali grasslands.

I walked the seventeen miles to the village, even though my hips were still sore from the shots from my malaria treatment. It was getting dark, and from my nomadic experience, I knew the night animals were coming out soon, hyenas in particular! Four months earlier, a young girl about ten years old was attacked and raped along this path, and she did not survive. That's all I could think of as I walked along the path. Nightfall was coming quickly and I still had a long way to go. I knew the path, including some short cuts through the bushes. I was walking as quickly as I could. I was still convalescent from malaria. I tried to stay in open land, but at times, the path went through wooded areas into remote places and around farmer's fields. It was the dry season, so there was nothing green, and the path was well worn.

When I got home, it was dark. From a distance, I could see the village with fires burning outside peoples' huts. Soon, I could hear animals and people as I got closer. I came to our hut and I was so glad to see.

"Oh, you look so good. You've gained weight and you have chubby cheeks." She happily said and hugged me. "I brought you sugar and tea, Grandma." I replied. Gladly she said, "Oh, you know what I like." I told her I left the rest of the gifts at the bus station, because I couldn't carry them. The next day, my dear Uncle Ahmed walked back to the bus stop and got the rest of my items from the store owner.

Right away, I was back to my responsibilities. That same evening, I did my chores and prepared to take the goats and sheep out to graze the next morning. My routine began again! At that point, I was upset at my mother for making me come back to the village. I even hoped I would end up with bad malaria again, so I could go back to Mogadishu and stay with my mother.

A few weeks later, due to the terribly dry weather, we had to move out into the grasslands to graze the animals again. Grandmother, Ahmed and I gathered all the cows, sheep and goats and headed out. This time, I would not ride on the donkey cart. I had to walk alongside the animals to help keep them in line. During the whole journey, my thoughts wandered back to my mother's home. I couldn't stop thinking about the nice bed, with sheets and pillows, the running water, and the children playing outside. Most of all, my thoughts went to my mother and how much I wanted her in my life so I could be like the rest of the children. I walked alongside the animals, dust wafting through the air from their hooves, through the parched and dry countryside, looking for green grass. I thought to myself, "They are my family and loved ones, and this is my life."

"What lies behind you and what lies in front of you, pales in comparison to what lies inside of you?" - Ralph Waldo Emerson

Chapter 5

FEMALE CIRCUMCISION

"Don't judge me for others' mistakes."

When I tell people that I am from Somalia, sometimes I am asked, "Did you have the procedure? The one where they cut the female part." I answer, "Yes, I did." I can see their face turning red, as if they ate hot pepper. "Do you mind explaining what it is like? Is there anesthesia or medication, so you don't feel the pain?" they ask.

The procedure took place in our village and many villages around the world. Somalia has been described by anthropologists as "the land of sewn women". Somalia has the highest percentage of female circumcision in all the countries. Millions of women have undergone the procedure for hundreds of years. In my opinion, the words "procedure" or "surgery" are too civilized for what happens. "Mutilation" is a more accurate term.

Each year in mid-summer, between planting and harvesting, the girls between by the age of seven and nine are gathered for their circumcision also called "pharaonic circumcision" after the pharaoh who, thousands of years ago, began that practice. It started when the pharaoh went on a long journey and did not want his wife to cheat on him. He had her genital area sewn together except for a small opening to urinate. This is how girls grow up to seven until they are married and her husband forcefully "opens" her genitals on their wedding night.

The procedure is performed by an older woman in our village. She was known for her fierce facial look. If you were a girl, the woman's looks alone will intimidate you. We would almost pee on ourselves when we saw her. The village ladies would be the woman's helpers. They would gather together at a central area with a few common huts that were used for community events. Every young girl that needed the procedure would be brought to them. Each year, I would hear it happen; the screams would sound through the entire village. I will never get those screams out of my head; I can still hear them if I close my eyes whenever I reminisce it. The young girls were forced to wait in line outside one of the common huts, waiting for their turn under the razor; until two older women come out and take them inside. I can just hear your inner voice now saying "I will run". Well, try and run if you can! There are women and men watching them; you would not go far. It was scary and awful. Yet, because of pressure and fear of being "different" from the other girls and women, everyone complied. It happened year after year, seasons after seasons, for all females in the country. Yes, it is still happening.

While standing there, they can hear the girl inside the hut, screaming and struggling. The pain was excruciating, no anesthesia and no sterile instruments. Are you feeling the chill and uneasiness? When the screaming stopped, soon the girl was carried out of the hut by two women with her legs tied together; blood covering her legs and dress, a shocking look in her eyes. The two women would place her under a tree with the other girls who had gone before her. They would wait until it was all over.

The next girl is usually frozen in fear, extremely reluctant to go inside. Soon, the screaming and crying would begin again, and the old woman would not stop until the job is done.

In the hut, on the ground on a wooden bed like a pallet, there is a cloth to soak the large puddle of blood left from the girl before. The clothes are piled up on the side until all the girls were circumcised.

After the old woman finished the procedure, she would stitch the girl's labia together using a thorn and thin pieces of cloth. She leaves an opening where urine can be released; a stick was placed at the opening of the girl's urethra to make sure it wasn't accidentally sewn shut during the stitching. The skin is to grow together except for a small opening. It's to stay this way until the girl's wedding night, when her husband will reopen it by force. If her husband is not able to open it during his attempts at intercourse, then he is labeled as "weak."

It takes about eight to twelve weeks for the wound to heal. During this time, she will lay in her family's hut on her wooden cot, with her legs still tied together. She is forced to relieve herself there; it's to be cleaned up by the women of the family. To minimize the need to urinate or defecate, no food is allowed. She can have only sips of water or milk. After two weeks, the girls are taken back to the old woman's hut to be inspected. If something doesn't look the way it should, then the procedure is repeated.

Chapter 6

THE NOMAD'S LIFE

The nomadic life consists in living with no fixed abode, herding the animals from pasture to pasture throughout the seasons. Spending my life growing up in our village and isolated from society, has made it challenging for me to be assertive. I couldn't tell my grandmother and uncles that I didn't want to herd the animals. I was afraid to be out by myself as I was the only girl among all those teenage boys and young men. Throughout the years, I never received praise for a job well done. There was never encouragement to think on my own or make my own decisions. I had become little more than a servant girl. I was beaten down, doing whatever I was told to do and doing it quietly.

When I was eight, another dry season hit Somalia; it was a serious one, with the grasslands drying up, turning brown and dusty. My grandmother and uncles decided that I was old enough to take the sheep and goats out as a nomad for several months without returning home, just like they did when I had malaria. It was the only way to keep the animals alive for any length of time. It had to be done or none of us would survive. This task was usually appointed to an older boy. It wasn't safe for a girl to be out by herself as a nomad. In our family, I was the boy or they just didn't care!

It was getting terribly dry and we were running out of places to graze the animals. One day my grandmother woke me up in the morning and said, "Habibo, I want you to learn how to take the sheep and goats out by yourself. They need to be brought to where there's rain and grass. We have relatives that we want you to go with to graze the sheep and goats."

My heart sank as I thought to myself, "Oh not again. I have to leave home and be out in the wild for half a year with people I don't even know?" The fears of being beaten up and raped were ever present on my mind. Regardless, I didn't argue with her. I was good at keeping my feelings inside and doing what I was told. My uncle, Ahmed arranged for me to take the herd along with our relatives, a man and his wife with their nephew, Sabriye. They were nomads; they spent all their time out wandering the grasslands, with no permanent home or village to live in, always in pursuit of green pastures.

Off we went on the nomadic adventures with the herd. The land was parched and dry; it hadn't rained for quite some time. The sheep and goats had little to eat as we walked. Each night, we slept on the ground with the herd gathered around us for safety while keeping an eye out for the hyenas. The next day, we continued walking. Shortly after, we arrived in a village where my uncle knew some relatives. They welcomed us and Ahmed introduced me, saying, "This is your cousin Habibo. She'll be staying with you, if that's alright, and she'll take care of our herd." After some greetings and discussion, as I stood there dumbfounded, Ahmed said good bye to me. He told me to make sure not so lose any of the herd. I can still see him walking away through the grassy field, leaving me behind with the herd and a family I had never met before. What else can I say order than nodding. I was so shocked and speechless.

At eight years, old, I had never been out on my own like this before for such a long a time. No other eight-year-old girl that I know had done that before. Even the boys, when out as nomads, were at least fourteen or fifteen years old, and they could defend themselves against wild animals and marauders.

My uncle left me with the family, father, stepmother and their son Sabriye. Sabriye and I ended up spending our time grazing the herds together. His stepmother was very unkind, always screaming at us and her husband. She was difficult to stay with because she seemed very unhappy and was taking it out on us. I tried to avoid the stepmother as much as I could. Her husband very quiet and he barely spoke. I assumed he learnt it was safer that way. I quickly learned that same lesson.

There was no solid food, so we were always hungry, except when we found fruits or roots as we walked the herd. She made porridge for her and her husband, but not for us. The cow's milk was precious to her because she would make butter out of it. It was easy for us to go up to a goat, lift up one of their back legs, grab their breast and squirt their milk in our mouth. It was gross, thick as half and half milk, with a strong taste to it. Most westernized people would find it distasteful or revolting, but when you're hungry for days, you will enter a survival mode and eat and drink whatever is at the reach of hands. Sometimes we switched from goat to cows and drink their milk.

My memories of this time are mostly sad and pitiful. I had no control of my life, no idea of what the future holds me. My future was goats, cows, grasslands, year in, year out. It was hard making friends because as nomads, we were moving around with no fixed abode. Wherever the heard could get some grassland, was our temporary residence. My world was evolving around the herd. I stayed with this family for three months. The stepmother got more and more hateful as time went on; she would scream at us, even when we hadn't done anything wrong. Sabriye and I just tried to make the best of the situation. Sometimes, that's all you can do. We wandered many miles, walking and talking, keeping the herd together.

At a particular morning, as we came down the mountainside, Sabriye was ahead of me, down the mountain leading the herd, while I took up the rear. Working my way through the rocks and down the rough terrain, I hit a rock, fell and rolled down few feet till my body slammed on a big rock that held my steep fall. I badly sprained my ankle and bruised my left hip. Sabriye couldn't hear my scream. When he finally realized, I wasn't with him, he came back up and helped me scoot down the mountain on my bottom.

I couldn't walk due to the swelling; so Sabriye whistled   aloud, which is how the nomads communicate to one another. A young man on his camel came to help us.   The boy helped me up onto his camel, which was not easy as camels are very tall animals, about seven feet. I rode on its back, holding onto the hump all the way back to the tent. It's a long way down off a camel's back. I spent the rest of the day back at the camp, lying outside, tending to myself. The following day, he and I went out again with the animals. This time, I had a limp to deal with.

Life went on this way for several months.

Finally, Uncle Ahmed came back to get me. I was so glad to see him and go back home. It had been hard work sleeping on the ground every night, getting yelled at by the step mother, and having very little to eat, but I made it. I learned that, as humans, we can endure a lot. In the morning, we gathered the herd together and started our walk back to the village, where life would resume its normal routine. I never appreciated "the normal routine" as much as when my time out with Sabriye and his family was over.

Chapter 7

DEEPEST DESPAIR

"No one's life is a smooth sail; we all come into stormy weather. But it's this adversity - and more specifically our resilience - that makes us strong and successful" — *Tony Robbins*

As I turned twelve I overheard my grandmother and Uncle Ahmed talking about sending me out again in the field to graze the cows for months. Bad memories of my last experience, despite my friendship with Sabriye came flooding back; the loneliness, being afraid and hungry, and the difficult lifestyle as a nomad. Sure enough, my grandmother told me that I would have to take the cows.

I had no choice in the matter. I didn't voice my questions as to why Ahmed or my grandmother couldn't come along. By this time in my life, I just did what I was told. My spirit was broken. I was like a slave. I knew the cows were more important than me. I felt like no one cared whether I lived or died;

whether I was raped or murdered. As long as the cows were fed, it didn't matter how I felt or what I wanted. No one ever asked me what I wanted or needed. No one asked me if I wanted to go. No rest, no break, no one saying "You're tired today. Let me take the cows out and you rest." I never said the word "no" until I was seventeen years old.

Without protesting, my uncle, Ahmed and I packed up my meager belongings, which I carried on my back. Early one morning, I took all the cows and calves, and we started walking. We walked all day through dry and dusty land; no grass, the bushes were nothing but skeletons, and no water anywhere. We camped that night around a fire. The next day, we milked some of the cows to have something for breakfast, and walked for another whole day.

Walking with Ahmed, I fell into a deep despair. I didn't share any of my feelings with him. I couldn't. I remembered feeling like I didn't care anymore if I lived or died. I was a beaten down spirit, desperate to get out of that living situation. The only way I had made it through life to this point, was to continue praying, "Help me, God! Something needs to change?" The only option for me was to hope for a marriage to continue the same lifestyle. I had very bad feelings about my mother and father; they had the resources to help me, but didn't. I thought about the other village girls who were so much better off than I was. They had parents, they didn't have to be nomads by themselves, they didn't do farm chores, and they weren't out walking behind a herd of cattle through the barren land. I wasn't like the other girls.

Through words of mouth from nomads we met along the way, we found the hut of the family we were looking for around 8 o'clock on the second night. It was a mother and her three teenage sons at home for the night sitting around a fire. The sons were a few years older than me; their father had died several years earlier. They were true nomads, constantly having to move their animals from one rainy season to the next, all throughout Somalia; going to town only once in a great while to sell their animals and buy few supplies. Ahmed spoke with the mother and introduced me, asking if I could stay near them and take our cattle out. He assured her I would find my own places, so as not to interfere with their herds. She agreed. I could see mischief in the eyes of the three boys when they found that a twelve-year-old girl would be joining them. By this time in my life, I came to recognize that look and I learned to always be on my guard. My heart sank once again; I knew I would be fighting to keep from being molested. I would be with them for several months.

None of them greeted me with warmth. They were a bit odd; nice, but not cheerful. Being out by themselves their whole lives made them different than village people. The oldest son, Hassan, welcomed me. He was kind and somewhat nice. It seemed like he took the place of the father.

Ahmed and I settled the cattle down where we would sleep with them in the sand outside the hut, on the ground, near the fire. I had one wrap that I used as my blanket the whole time I was there. My bed remained a little spot outside the hut, where I made a bed of grass and leaves.

When Ahmed left early the next morning, before sunrise, all he said was "Take care of yourself." And off he went. I wanted to cry, but I held in until I was by myself.

That morning, the three boys and I took the animals far from their tent to graze in the grasslands. It was a pretty impressive herd. We left early that morning, as I did each morning thereafter. It was barely bright enough to see. We had walked for two hours or so, the animals grazing along the way. They all mixed together. The four of us, one in front, the rest on the sides and the rear, kept them going. Each one of us had our long shepherd's stick. The animals stuck together. They're smart that way; knowing it would mean death for them to wander off by themselves. It was very dry - dry grass everywhere, coming way up above our knees. They showed me an area for my cows to graze and taught me whistles to make as a signal between us if I got lost. They warned me not to wander off too far. That first time, I was cautious and stayed close to what looked familiar to me, while they went off in different directions.

I spent that day afraid. I didn't know who was in the area. I didn't know what kind of animals I would encounter. I did know that there would be no other girls to befriend. I felt hopeless. I thought, "Why me?" I was sad and that was when I cried.

The nomad guys were known to be dangerous, rough and aggressive, living out in the bush all the time. Rumor had it that the camel's milk, which they drank, was an aphrodisiac, which made them even more aggressive. I was worried to be raped or lose my cows. I didn't know which would be worse. Probably losing the cows, or even one cow!

The second day I was there, I went with Hassan to the watering spot, where everyone took their herds to drink. We left before sunrise and walked for at least half the day with one hundred and fifty cows between us. All we had to eat that morning was milk, which wasn't very filling. In fact, that's what I had to eat every day, with nothing else except the dried fruit, nuts and roots I found. I got used to being hungry, and living off of nothing but milk.

We got to the well at high noon and had to wait our turn. This was the central gathering spot for everyone. There were several nomads there with their herds at any given time during the day. It was a busy place; cows bellowing, bells ringing, nomads yelling, dust filling the air. When we arrived, there were about forty other people. There was even a little makeshift café to buy tea and bread.

When it was our turn, Hassan showed me how to draw the water out of the well with a bucket tied to a rope. We poured it into a big tank and let the cows, four or five at a time, drink to their fill. Of course, the law of nature governed, as the stronger cows got the water first, pushing their way in to the trough. Finally, the weaker ones would get their drinks, also.

It took us over an hour to water all the cows. We pulled the buckets up for ourselves; poured it over ourselves, clothes and all, and washed all the dust and dirt off. I wasn't wearing a head covering because I wasn't married, so I washed my hair with the water. Hassan was nice to me, and I liked him. We cleaned up and cooled off, then started heading back towards home. It would take the better part of the afternoon to get back to the hut.

After that, I took my herd of cows to the well by myself. Often times, there were others nomads there before me, so I had to wait my turn. Sometimes people were nice and let me go ahead of them or they'd help me lift the water out of the well and pour it into the trough. Other times, they'd take advantage of me, pushing me and my herd out of the way, harassing me and calling me names, or just trying to intimidate me. Each time I went there, I would hope there wouldn't be rough people around the well. This was also my time to cool off and wash all the dust and dirt off myself and my clothes. If there was trouble around, I'd just water the cows and leave as soon as I could.

Each day, the same scenario repeats Surely enough, the cows knew where to go, so I would just follow along with my stick, making sure they stayed together until we found grass patches for them to eat on. I had no idea that war was brewing in the country. I didn't realize how civil war would change my life; it was an answer to my prayers.

While out by myself, if I saw camel boys and their herds, I'd hide myself in the bushes and trees or in some ditch, so they wouldn't see me. I spent much of my time like this, hiding in the woods being afraid. I avoided them at all costs; they were older, stronger and aggressive. Anytime I heard someone coming with their herd, I would climb a tree or some tall bush to see if I knew them. It always made me nervous. If there were several boys or men, they'd be bolder. Many times, I'd have to hide in the trees, so they wouldn't find me; otherwise, there was nothing I could do. The boys would come my way and ask if I was there by myself. I always made up a story that someone was around, like my uncle or brothers; that they were just over the hillside and would hurt them if they touched me.

Those boys had little contact with the outside world, no education, and no law to abide by. It was the law of nature. If only one boy tried to get me, I would fight and sometimes win. I always had my stick with me, and I would put up a good fight. I would hit them with my stick right in the crotch. If there was more than one or a group, which happened often, I wouldn't fight. What was going to happen was inevitable. I was thankful that I hadn't reached maturity yet and couldn't get pregnant. Sadly, I had to be on the alert every day and ready to fight at any moment. It was difficult to sit, watch the cows and relax. At any moment, I could be attacked. To this day, I must admit, I am on alert. I am not necessarily afraid of being molested, but my inner being is on alert. It's hard for me to relax, but I am working on it.

Each night at the camp, we would keep the fire going all night to ward off wild animals, so it was nice and warm to lay by the fire. The three boys and I slept outside, while their mother slept inside the hut. Apparently, she wasn't concerned with me being out there with her sons, because I could have slept in the hut with her. The animals were in their makeshift corrals, but they could still be attacked, especially the young ones. We could hear the wild animals out in the grasslands and forests howling and growling;

hyenas, jackals and sometimes a lion, even though they were scarce. If we kept a fire going and stayed close to it with the herd, we were all safe.

I was so afraid, sleeping outside with, not only the wild animals, but the three teenage boys. I knew this was a dangerous situation. It wasn't often that they had a twelve-year-old girl sleeping outside with them by the fire, while their mother slept soundly inside the tent. Before sleeping, I wrapped my little shawl around me, laid on the ground and tied my legs together with a rope that I had woven together out of long grass. That way, they would not be able to rape me easily. I slept this way the whole time I was there because I could not trust the boys due to my previous experiences. Have you ever tried to sleep with a rope tied around your legs? Probably not, but maybe you could try it sometime – for the whole night!

Most of the time, my days were spent in the sunshine, making ropes or dolls out of sticks and grass, or trying to find dry fruits. Sometimes, I'd just sit there and cry. I felt out of place, tired, hungry, and dirty. I knew I had lice, but I couldn't get rid of them. I would sing whatever songs I could remember, thinking that perhaps it was soothing the cows. I thought about my life. I thought about how no one cared for me. I thought about getting married and having children of my own someday. I kept thinking there had to be more in this world for me. I hated my situation, stuck out in the grasslands, with nothing but hyenas, jackals and older boys leering at me and trying to get me down on the ground for their own pleasure. I lived like this for several months, never knowing when I would be going home. I kept hearing that it hadn't rained back home, so I knew it could be a long time. However, the cows were doing well and Grandmother was happy.

To make matters worse, there were weird people going from hut to hut at night to steal or rape - night stealers or night rapist, we would call them. One night, several weeks after I got there, we heard yelling and crying coming from another family's tent, not too far from ours. Hassan said, "Stay here, I'll check it out." He ran to the tent where the screams were coming from. It was a mother with her two daughters and son who lived there. There was a big strong guy who entered the hut, trying to take some sugar and food from them. Before he left, he tried to rape the woman. She kicked him, and as he was trying to get away, she grabbed his ankle and wouldn't let him go. He kicked and punched, dragging her fifty feet or more away from her hut, but she refused to give up. Several guys from other tents in the area came to rescue, arrested the guy and tied him to a tree. In the next morning, we all came to check him out. The men tried to teach him a lesson;

they beat him up badly and told him to leave. Hopefully, he heeded their warning.

"There is a powerful driving force inside every human being that, once unleashed, can make any vision, dream, or desire a reality." Tony Robbins

---

During this time in my life, I lost a lot of weight due to tapeworms, in addition to the head lice. You could tell by looking at me that I was not very happy. I was exhausted, worn out, tired of being afraid and fighting abuse. I was so lonely. This was the darkest part of my life. At twelve-years-old, a point of despair, I almost gave up. The dawn comes after the darkest part of the night, never before.

As time went on, I became more of a loner. That's how I survived; sticking to myself, keeping my nose clean, putting on a tough exterior and never asking for help. The boys didn't talk to me or have much to do with me. Scared and nervous, I didn't welcome any friendship from them. Feeling alone and helpless in such a fearful situation caused me to become very withdrawn and reserved.

Being a nomad, however, had its payoff for me in the long run. I learned how to be strong and assertive. I learned how to depend on myself, how to be on my guard, and to never trust anyone and to survive. I continued to have trouble being able to relax and be comfortable. In a way, I am still a nomad protecting myself. I learned to be stoic and unemotional. I told myself, "This is what you have to do now. You have no choice, so just do it." That attitude helped me as I traveled to America. Starting a life in America and becoming successful is not easy, but I did it.

One day, my uncle, Abdi, unexpectedly came to see how I was doing. I was surprised to see him, as he rarely left the farm. I was glad to see him, even if he was constantly criticizing and making fun of me. I welcomed him, thinking maybe my time out there was over and I'd be going back to the village. After seeing the cows were in good shape, he told me he would see me later, and left, turning around and walking back to the village. He didn't even check on my well-being.

My spirit was close to be completely broken. I know how a prisoner feels, locked up in a terrible place, with no hope of getting out and having to fight for their life every day. I see why people just give up and let life treat them at will. I felt so disheartened. I needed to go home. I felt my life had turned into a nightmare.

Life went on; day after day, the same story. Two months later, my other uncle, Ahmed came to see me. He took one look at me, ignoring the cows, and said, "I do not like what I see, Habibo. We're going back to the village; the cows can eat corn stalks. You're so thin and you have lice." I was so happy! Ahmed was always my savior. He was the only one who cared for me. He was the father I never had. Oddly enough, I had mixed feelings about going back to life in the village. It wasn't much better, but I had to go.

To this day, I question how they could have done that to a young girl. I still ask myself, "How was that acceptable?" I didn't have anyone there to say, "Get this girl out of here; get her into school; give her some decent clothes." I wish I didn't have to accept that the cows were more important than I was. For so long, I hoped there were some feelings for me, but, that wasn't the case. A friend of mine later told me, "Habibo, it wasn't acceptable. It's as simple as that. It just wasn't acceptable." That's a hard thing to take, but it happens to us. We're not always guaranteed to have people around to care for us; sometimes we have just the opposite. It's important to care for ourselves and not to give up hope.

Ahmed and I took the cows and walked one whole day towards the village, and camped overnight on the way back. I was happy to leave the grasslands. The next day, we milked the cows for our breakfast and walked the entire day and evening.

Finally, we arrived at the village around 9 o'clock, completely exhausted and barely able to walk anymore. We were covered in dust, dirt and lice. When I came into my grandmother's hero and into her hut, she did not even get up to greet me. She said, "Aren't you going to come over here and give me a hug?" I felt like I wasn't loved; I felt like I was just a farm hand. Putting the cows in their corral, I ate whatever was left for supper, fell on my bed and slept.

The next morning, before the sun came up, my grandmother woke me up, "Habibo, wake up. It's time to get up and get chores done. You must take the cows out today." I couldn't believe it. I was expected to get up and do the usual chores; make a fire, fetch water at the river, prepare breakfast and then, take the cows out to graze. I got up and did my chores.

Before I left with the herd, my grandmother did what she thought was best to get rid of the lice on my head. With a razor, she shaved my head and rubbed laundry detergent flakes into my scalp. That's how I went out that day. I was told to leave it on for a while and then rinse it off in the river. Later that day, I rinsed it off, but I got a terrible headache from the detergent. It was the worst headache I've ever had. It stayed with me the rest of the day and all night. I couldn't close my eyes and I felt like my head was about to burst out. I sat up all night by myself in the dark outside the hut.

The next morning, I was expected to take the cows out. My head was shaved like a man, so the other young people of the village laughed at me and called me names. They told me I was like a boy and made fun of me. I was so crushed. I thought I would never get married. No one in their right mind would ever love me. I looked so hideous. Slowly, my hair grew back.

I felt stronger after I survived the nomad experience by myself. I was soon the talk of the village. "Habibo took her grandma's cows out by herself." "Habibo took the cow's way out in the country for a long time." "Oh, she is strong." "She does anything she's asked to do." "She will make a good wife." I was praised for it. I proved myself.

I began to see that my life with my grandmother was temporary. My mind was made up. I was going to leave. I thought to myself "It will be over soon." So, I did what I could to look nice and continued my work.

Later that year, the dry seasons continued to be very harsh, so we had to move again to graze the animals. This time wasn't as bad because my grandmother and Ahmed came along. Perhaps Ahmed had something to do with that, after seeing what happened to me when I was out alone.

"Every day, we can either choose to be a victim or we can choose to live life victoriously." - Les Brown

We walked the animals all the way to the border of Ethiopia and stayed there for several months, camping from site to site. We brought barley, butter, milk, and tea. We camped close to the river, so we could get water for us and the animals. Ahmed always slept outside, but Grandma and I slept in the hut. This time, I took the goats and sheep, Ahmed took the cows, and Grandmother stayed behind with the younger calves, sheep and goats. This is one of the more pleasant memories of living with my grandmother. I think my grandmother realized that I was becoming a woman and, whether she liked it or not, she would lose me soon enough. I think, deep down, my grandmother did not want a village life for me. I think that is why she would kick out the boys when they came to our hut to talk to me. It was like a vacation being a way from uncle Abdi. Meeting new friends was fantastic.

Looking back, I think things changed between me, my grandmother and my uncles after my experience taking the cows out by myself. I was older and ready for marriage. I was much stronger and sure footed than before. The nomadic experience, gave me a confidence I never had before.

In my mind, it clarified what I wanted out of life – and it wasn't life as I knew it!

This is when I had my first marriage offer. I was thirteen, and an eighteen-year-old wanted to marry me. The request came from his father to my grandmother. He came to our hut and said, "Oh, your granddaughter, Habibo, is so well behaved and works so hard. I never see her complain, even at night when she's with the cows. She's always working. I would like my son to marry her." "No, Habibo is not ready for marriage" my Grandmother replied.

I think my grandmother and my uncles weren't ready to let me go. They wanted me to help with the work. Then the father proposed to my grandmother, saying, "Well, then, how about if I marry you?"

My grandmother said, "No way."

Chapter 8

NO LONGER A NOMAD

"With everything that has happened to you, you can either feel sorry for yourself or treat what has happened as a gift. Everything is either an opportunity to grow or an obstacle to keep you from growing. You get to choose." – Wayne W. Dyer

In the fall of 1995, after several cycles of nomadic life and increased fighting amongst the tribes, my grandmother received a letter from my mother, asking her to send me to Nairobi, Kenya where she live with her four children. They moved there for safety reasons because of the war in Somalia. The letter was given to a man who had come from Nairobi. He gave it to a local farmer who was selling his herd in Beledwayne. He, then, delivered it to us in the village.

I wasn't aware that we had received a letter and that my departure was being discussed. I was getting to the age where I could be married soon, as thirteen or fourteen is prime time for a Somali girl to be married. I knew this would be my ticket out. Several of the boys from the village were, in a sense, courting me. We would get together and talk;

spending time together to see if we liked each other. My grandmother and uncles realized they were going to lose me before too long. Once I got married, I would be moving in with my husband on his father's farm and working there.

My grandmother told me, "Habibo, your mother would like you to go to Nairobi and help her. We are considering letting you go, but haven't decided yet." I got excited at the thought that I'd be able to leave the village and the work I was required to do with little or no thanks. I prayed that they would allow me to leave and that my life would change. Just the thought of being with my mother and four siblings, to me, would be like going to paradise, even if it were in a poor section of Nairobi with little or no money. Anything seemed better than the continued hard labor I endured. Finally, few days, my grandmother told me they decided it would be better to let me go and be with my mother and four siblings, who I had never met. I was ecstatic to hear that. At last, I would be leaving. It was hard for me to imagine a life outside the village; where herding animals, working in the fields and going out as a nomad was all I knew of. I didn't know much about the outside world except for few weeks I spent with my mother in Mogadishu when I had malaria. However, I liked what I saw. I knew Nairobi was a very large city with cars and lights and lots of people, but it made me nervous thinking about it. All that matters were a chance, even if it were a small chance, at something better than what I had had. I was the labor girl. I couldn't read, I couldn't write and the only language I knew was Somali. All I knew was the hard life of the village. Now that I look back, my prayers were answered the day we received that letter from my mother. My life has never been the same since.

With permission from my grandmother and uncles, it didn't take me long to prepare to leave. I didn't have many belongings besides my tire sandals, two skirts, and a torn-out scarf covering my head. I had no money and I didn't know where Kenya was or what Nairobi looked like but I was willing and anxious to go. I was ready to find a different future for myself. I was anxious to see my mother and meet the siblings I never met before. Being part of a family with brothers and sisters was one of my biggest dreams. It was the one thing I wanted the most, to belong to something or someone. I was also nervous to go because I had only been with my mother for a few weeks and that was when I was seven with malaria. I wasn't sure how we would get along. Most importantly, I was joyful to finally leave the criticism and poor treatment I received, along with the stern discipline of my grandmother. The truth is, I was afraid of her, as she was quick to whip me and yell at me - she was one tough chick!

It wasn't long after, probably a week, when the day came for us to leave. My uncle, Ahmed and grandmother took me to Beledwayne. We left early in the morning, before sunrise, to catch the bus. I did not know where my other uncles were; probably sleeping in their own tent, but there were no goodbyes between us. So, we left and walked to the bus stop about twenty-six miles away.

The walk to the bus was nice. I was glad Uncle Ahmed was there to take me; his voice was always so gentle. It felt different this time because there was no herd, just us both walking to the bus stop and we had time to talk to each other as we walked. If it weren't for Ahmed, there wouldn't have been much love for me growing up in the village. I'll never forget his kindness. Not once did he raise his voice at me, except in his frustration when I lost a sheep in the river, and he had to jump in, despite the crocodiles, to save it. I think I would raise my voice, as well, in that situation.

The bus announced itself with plumes of dust we could see off in the distance, as it sped towards us on the dirt road. I had my little bag in my hand and I was wearing my good dress, anxious to be going off to the big city.

The bus was full of people: mothers with children, old folks, young people, all going to the city as well. We got on, squeezing our way to a seat;

Grandma and I in one, Ahmed in another, and off we went to Beledwayne, which took about another three hours. I then realized I was leaving my life in the village forever. It was bitter sweet; I wouldn't be seeing my favorite animals, walking the path to the river to fetch water, or living the simple life of the village. It was scary because this is all I knew. I thought to myself, "I should have run off with a boy when I had chance and never come back."

When we arrived, we walked to Ahmed's friend's house. His name was Nabil, where my grandmother and I stayed. Ahmed stayed with another family due to lack of space at Nabil's house. We stayed there for about a week while we waited for a cargo plane to come from Nairobi. There were no passenger planes in and out of Beledwayne, only planes that carried various kinds of cargo. If you could bribe the pilot, you could catch a ride to Nairobi, although it was illegal. An aunt of mine in Nairobi paid a pilot for my passage, so when he delivered his cargo to Beledwayne, he would transport me back to Nairobi. We had to wait until his plane came with only a vague sense that it would be soon.

There in Beledwayne, it was one of the first times I had ever seen lights, cars, trucks, and regular houses. It was such a contrast from the country village I came from. Ahmed came to visit each day as we waited for the plane to arrive. We had no money, so we couldn't do much. I don't know why we didn't sell a sheep or goat to have some money, but we didn't; it didn't make any sense to me anyway. I was disappointed that they didn't buy me something nicer to wear. The other girls of my age had more attractive clothes and I was self-conscious.

Finally, a week later, the plane landed with its load of "khat", which is like tobacco with an added stimulant. We met with the pilot who told us that he was returning to Nairobi the very next day. Early the next morning, we arrived at the airport to find the plane and pilot. I bid farewell to my grandmother and thanked her for all she'd done for me. I also thought about how much I had done for her, but all she said was, "Be good, Habibo." I said goodbye to Ahmed and climbed on board the plane. I looked back and saw him standing there, with his long robe and cheerful face. I didn't see him again until many years later.

There was a business woman who needed to go to Kenya on the plane, as well. It was just the business woman, the pilot, and I. It was my first time on an airplane. I was petrified. I just knew we would crash before we got there. There were no seats or a toilet. We sat on the floor. When the plane got bumpy with turbulence, we had to hang on to cargo bags. The pilot was walking around in the plane. I thought, "I am going to die soon." To help calm me down, the woman with me gave me a piece of gum, real gum, which I had never had before. I was used to the gum we made from a certain trees' juice and we chewed on. The gum she gave me had two wrappers, which I did not understand. I removed the outside paper wrap and put the piece in my mouth with the silver wrapping. It is so funny, now that I look back on it. "No, you have to take the silver wrap off, silly girl." The lady said.

I chewed it for a little while, but spit it out before too long. It wasn't as good as the gum I found on trees.

After an hour or so, we had to stop at the border of Kenya and Somalia to fuel up. The lady and I stayed in the back of the plane since we weren't supposed to be there. The landing was frightening. I thought the plane was going to tear apart or run into the buildings because we were going so fast. However, we were fine. We took off again and flew for maybe another hour before landing at a small airport in Nairobi around 5 o'clock in the evening. It was heavily raining by then.

With the civil war happening in Somalia, it was dangerous to cross country lines without transfer papers. If you were caught, you'd be put in jail with no way out, except to bribe your way. I had no papers with me to show the officials at the airport, so the woman I flew with agreed to tell them that I was her daughter to get me through the gates without any trouble. She said, "Just pretend you are with me."

We got off the plane and slipped in with some other people walking towards the airport, pretending to be part of their group. It was a gated area; uniformed men with guns were standing all around. Security was high due to the war. I was so afraid. I had a sinking feeling that, with so many men there, I'd get raped again. I just kept my eyes down and didn't look up at any of them. I felt the men's eyes on me and my memories came flooding back of fight or flight. I felt they could look at me and know that I was illegal; I thought it was written all over my face. We made it through the gates and into the airport, thanks to the woman I was traveling with. I don't know what would have happened if I had been by myself. I had no idea where to go. Without papers, I probably wouldn't have been allowed to leave the gates. I looked around the airport and realized no one was there to pick me up.

I am sure the woman I was with, felt sorry for me, thinking, "What kind of a family is this child from?" To be honest, I asked myself the same question. The woman told me she had friends in Nairobi and I could stay with them until we got hold of my mother. I agreed, having no other choice. We waited for a taxi. We were wet from the rain. I was scared, cold, and tired. Finally, the taxi arrived. We were in for a bumpy ride. The man was a very poor driver; swerving in and around the traffic, going so fast. Of course, I wasn't accustomed to riding in the city. It is different from riding on a donkey cart. Our taxi went through the streets of Nairobi, which was much bigger than anything I had ever seen or imagined. Everything was so fast and busy. I was confused and bewildered. It was totally different to what I was used to - cement and tar, buildings with lights, cars and lots of traffic, people everywhere!

We finally arrived at the friend's house, and I was so glad. Providentially, the woman's friend was from my tribe – the Hawaadle tribe, and, oddly enough, she knew my aunt who had arranged for my flight. The woman's friend even had my aunt's phone number. It's in times like this when my faith was strengthened; moments when, against the odds, things started working out. The woman's friend called my aunt and told her I had arrived. My aunt wasn't at the airport because she didn't know when the plane would arrive. That's how it is when you bribe a pilot.

I went to bed that night feeling tired from the plane ride, the men with guns at the airport, and the taxi ride. I needed to sleep badly. It was a nice house. It was comfortable, with bunk beds and nice pillows. It was the pillows that always impressed me when I went to the city. All I had was a rolled-up piece of cloth or my arm to lay my head on. They had a flush toilet, which I had never seen before. In the village, we just went out into the bush to relieve ourselves. I didn't understand the flushing part of the toilet.

I slept well. It was the first time I had been in a real bed since I was seven. You can imagine how I felt with clean sheets, blankets and a pillow - with a pillow case! It's funny what we take for granted, but these things, to many people in the world, are a major luxury that only rich people enjoy. I find it odd that people complain when they have a nice life.

The next day, my aunt's husband came to get me. It wasn't until 11 o'clock at night that he arrived. I was scared. I didn't know where we were going and I didn't know this man. We drove for a while, until he had to stop at a restaurant for some reason. He told me, "Wait here." I stood in the corner, not knowing what to do. The room was full of men sitting around, eating and talking. I started to get uncomfortable and worried that the man had abandoned me there. I wanted to run and find a way back to my grandma's village. I was terrified! Finally, he came back. I was so hungry, but with no money, I couldn't buy food. I wished I had some cow's milk with me.

When we arrived, my mother was waiting for me outside the gate in front of the blue colored hotel where she was staying. It was the first time I saw her in several years. I was very excited. She came out of the gate and we were both so overwhelmed with joy, we ran to each other, hugging, kissing and crying. It was the most amazing feeling. She took me up to her room, where we started talking and crying some more. I saw my little brothers and sisters: Naima was four years old, Nura was three, Halima was two, and Mohamed was five months old. I was so happy. I kissed and hugged them, lifted them up and played with them. We talked all night till four in the morning and then I slept past noon.

I was in for a shock, as life in Nairobi with my mother, brother and sisters was chaotic and tenuous. With the civil war in full force, hundreds and thousands of families, men, women and their children, young people and old alike, flooded into Kenya, escaping for their lives. I was expecting something like where my mother lived in Mogadishu, when I stayed with her over there; however, the war changed everything. The city had swelled to more than twice its size, and people were moving about everywhere, coming in from all over. We had no papers allowing us to be in the country and no money. Without papers, we had to hide all the time, being very careful when we left the apartment so we didn't get caught. The police came every night, knocking on doors and demanding to see papers. If you didn't have papers, you were taken to jail. Bribery was the only way out. After few weeks of living in hiding and fear in my mother's motel room, she thought it would be best for us to leave Nairobi.

I didn't realize we would be going to a refugee camp, but my mother knew, and she knew it was our only option.

My mother and I, with my four siblings, packed up a few things and left one night around midnight, when the city quieted down and there weren't as many soldiers and police around. We were so afraid of being caught, watching over our shoulders all the time, and trying to carry the little ones and our few belongings. We took a taxi to the bus station because we heard there was a bus leaving around 2 o'clock in the morning. Thankfully, we got on the bus without any trouble.

We traveled on the bus the whole night. The children slept as much as they could, but the seats were close together and the bus was crowded. We were all so tired with little or no sleep. The next morning, we got to Mombasa, the second largest city in Kenya. From there, we had to walk with the kids and our belongings to an old refugee camp called Utaango. It took us about three hours to get there. Utaango was a refugee camp that was about to be closed. I found out we were not going to stay there. We were told there would be a bus to take people to another camp, and we had to wait a day or two before leaving

Utaango was overcrowded and very unsanitary; it was disgusting. We found a friend of my mother's living in a tent, so we stayed with her for a day and night. The camp was built in a wet, rainy part of Kenya, much like a rain forest. It was muddy, with tents set up in the middle of the mud. There were lots of people, many sick and dying. It was infested from all the people trying to live there. There were feces and rotten food all around. The camp was full of cholera, hepatitis A, typhoid, and malaria. Children and old folks were dying every single hour. Before we left Nairobi, we heard that Utaango was vile. We were told to buy socks at the second-hand store before we got there because there were worms crawling in the dirt that would try to burrow into the bottom of your feet. We had to keep socks on the kids' feet. It was the absolute worst of life.

The first night, my mother, brother and sisters slept inside the tent. The lady and I had to sleep outside on the ground with the worms. I was so afraid of them. I barely slept that night.

We woke up the next morning to find the buses weren't going to leave for another day, so we had to stay. It was one of the worst days of my life. Everything was wet and dirty, people were coughing, sick and dying everywhere. Little children were sitting, staring with huge eyes and no muscle on their bones, with large stomachs and sticks for legs. I was so worried that one of us would catch a disease. The constant threat of worms burrowing into your feet was enough to make you crazy. It was something out of a nightmare.

The next day, we left with as many people from the camp that could fit on the bus. For two days, we rode through the open grasslands to the other side of Kenya. It was the most tiresome and annoying experience I have ever been through. We only stopped at night when the bus driver pulled over in the desert so everyone could get out and sleep on the ground. I was so tired, dirty, hungry and worn out. It was like something out of a movie. We were struggling for our lives, escaping a war-ravaged country with no place to go. Every one of us had been uprooted from our homes with nothing in our name, except for a few pieces of clothing and whatever we could grab. I could see the fear and fatigue in peoples' eyes. It was a very sad thing as we made our way to another refugee camp – the largest in the entire world: Dadaab

Chapter 9

DADAAB LARGEST REFUGEE CAMP

We arrived at Dadaab during the day. The camp began in 1992 after General Barre was ousted from power, and everyone fled Somalia. It has three main sites, which were built to hold a total of 90,000 refugees. By the time, we arrived there in 1995, there were almost 150,000 refugees. Today, there are over 500,000. I got off the bus and looked over the landscape; I could see thousands and thousands of people, tents after tents, across the land, which was flat and dusty, barren and wide open – nothing you could graze your animals on.

We got off the bus and stood in line with the other people. We checked in at the reception center manned by people from the United Nations. They took our names down and gave us a large tarp to make a tent, some corn, oil, flour, several plastic jugs for us to fill with water at one of the wells, along with a little cart with wheel, and some mattresses. The camp was divided into sections in alphabetical order, and within each letters of the alphabet e were the subsections like, A-1, A-2, A-3 and so on. Each subsection had about ten families in it with their tents set up about fifty feet from each other. We were assigned to section F-4. The United Nations, which was running Dadaab, did not understand Somalia tribalism, and they mixed everyone together from many different tribes, making way to a tense situation.

With our tent and food, we took the little ones to find our site and set up a camp. The first day was busy. We went outside the camp to find branches and limbs for the inner structure of our tent and for fire wood. We went to fetch water, took care of the kids and met the people around us, as well. A large makeshift fence surrounded the camp to keep out marauders, rapists and robbers. The fence was only made of limbs and branches from trees in the area, and with little effort, could be broken through. Our tent site was near the big fence, so I had to separate some of the branches to get outside to find branches and firewood so we could cook our meals. That night, we all fell asleep so early. We were so tired from traveling for days, taking care of the little ones, getting into the camp and finding our way through it, not to mention two days at Tango. Soon, we got used to the camp.

Imagine being surrounded by thousands of Somali men, women and children, all having escaped their homeland, trying to survive in the middle of a vast, barren land. I was very intimidated at first. I had never been around so many people in such a large area. It was overwhelming. Many people were from the cities of Somalia. They were more educated and more sophisticated than I was. I felt belittled. I had very little self-confidence and less self-esteem, so it strained me from interacting with all the people. However, we had to survive, and I did what I had to do.

There were four wells and depending on where you tent is located, you could walk about two to reach one of the wells. Starting on the first day and every other day after that, I walked to the well closest to us, about a half hour walk, pulling the little cart with our four water containers, through the hot sand.

Each day, hundreds of people would also go to the well, so I had to start before dawn to avoid the line. There were fights in the line, mainly from women arguing and fighting over their place. Sometimes, the fights would get serious with knives and machetes. People would put their water tanks in front of each other or try to butt into line. The fights would break out and spread to families back in the camps with mothers, fathers, children and relatives fighting with some other families. Are we humans or animals? Soon, it would be one whole section of the camp against another, everyone with knives, sharp sticks or whatever else they could find to hurt each other. Many times, people were seriously hurt and had to be taken to the UN Center for medical for treatment. My best defense was not to fuss with people. If they wanted to break into line in front of me, I'd let them. For three years, I dealt with that precarious line. I was never sure when a fight would break out, as tempers flared and patience with life became scarce.

After getting our water, I'd make breakfast for us. Usually we'd have bread made from flour, water, and oil that we were given. Other times, we'd have ground corn and make a flat corn pancake out of it. Sometimes, I'd trade the corn with the neighbors for a little tea. Bartering was a way to survive since very few people had money to buy anything. We also had a type of pasta which I'd make from flour, water, oil and some powdered milk we'd get from the UN Center or from trading with one of the neighbors.

We washed the few cups or dishes that we had in a bucket, or rinse them, because all we had for soap were big bars cut from a large soap block. Our kitchen, outside our hut, was made of a small cubby, with bushes around it on three sides to keep the dust and sand out. For a fire pit, we had three rocks placed so we could build a fire in the middle; we placed our pots or pans on top of the rocks and cooked our food.

I cooked our food outside for three years, which wasn't unusual for me. We always cooked our meals outside in the village. I didn't know any different way. Sometimes my mother would be with us, sometimes not, as she'd often travel back to Nairobi to find money from relatives and friends, while I was left to look after the little ones.

Laundry was done by hand, three times per day, in cool water. Sometimes we had a bar of soap and sometimes we didn't. The kids had diarrhea the whole time we were there, so laundry was a daily issue. The bars of soap weren't like in America or western countries. There were bars rough cut from a big slab, which was then cut up into smaller pieces. I hung a line between the branches of the bushes around us to hang the clothes to dry. The clothes the kids had clothes called were "hudhay", or second hand stuff - colored t-shirts, no socks or underwear. Older kids would have sandals made from old tires. Younger kids went barefoot.

The kids didn't have much to occupy their time. They played in the sand around our tent, playing with empty bottles, sticks, rocks or, on occasion a scorpion! There were other children in our camp who my siblings would play with. They acted like nothing was wrong; life consisted of living in the camp with friends. Eventually our camp and the camps around us became like a little neighborhood within a large city. Many parts of it I never saw because it wasn't always safe to wander off by yourself in such a big place.

Health issues were prevalent – malaria, pin worms, tape worms, and malnourishment were part of daily life. Some of the children had cholera, sores and infections. My legs were always cut and sore. To this day, I have the scars to prove it. Scorpions were abundant and we were regularly bitten. If we were bitten, there were no doctors to take us to, so we just wrapped the bitten spot and hoped it would go away

Living there, life was always riddled with problems. Once a month, when we would pick up supplies of flour, corn and oil, fights would always break out. It was common for fights to occur with knives and often, someone got hurt and killed.

One of the biggest problems we had was finding firewood outside the camp. With so many people, with the need to cook by making a fire, the supply in the immediate vicinity of the camp quickly depleted. We went out in the bush to find firewood, which we only did during the daytime, never at night because it was dangerous. We went out in groups of three or four, many times walking several miles to find wood. The longer we lived at the refugee camp, the farther out we had to walk to find firewood. There were men and boys hiding outside the camp, who would live off of those living within the camp. They tried to rob you, rape you or sometimes, even kill you. Every week, we heard of these kinds of tragedies happening. Usually, if someone ventured out by themselves, they were easy prey. There were no police, so the people behaved and act at leisure.

At night, we could hear the animals howling outside the fence; hyenas and a large cat called a "duwaco". Occasionally, you would hear a gun shot or scream. The animals growled out in the bushes; we heard it and hoped it wouldn't get into our camp. My siblings were afraid at night so they slept close to me for comfort and I would always reassure them the animals wouldn't come in. Truthfully, I wasn't so sure. I was scared inwardly. At night, we were afraid because the "slichers", men and boys with guns and knives, would come in through the fence, go into tents, rape people and take jewelry or anything of value. Sometimes, they killed people. We'd hear guns popping and get news the next morning that the slichers were in this camp or that camp; luckily, they were never seen in our camp. During the night, if I had to relieve myself, I couldn't go because I was afraid of walking around in the bushes. I thought they might be around and kidnap or rape me. This wasn't much of an adjustment for me, because all my life in the village I had to be on guard for rape. I experienced it all the time as a nomad, being one of the only girl herding animals out in the grasslands.

Once a week, all the small children in the camp were taken to the UN Center, located in the middle of the camp, to be weighed and checked for diseases. Our section of Dadaab, F-4, went on

Wednesdays. I carried my six months old sister, Sahra, on my chest and two-year old brother, Mohamed, one on my back. They were plagued by diarrhea, making it a mess just to get to the center. It was about two miles away from our tent. I had to walk through the hot sand, so deep that my feet would sink in, making it very hard to walk. I made this trek twice a week so UN volunteers from other countries could poke Sarah and Mohamed's fingers to check their iron levels and weigh them, trying to keep ahead of malnutrition. They gave us cookies, crackers and, based upon their weight, additional dried milk, oil, corn and rice to take back to our camp, which we were so grateful. Despite the treks to the UN Center and the additional food, my brother and sisters became malnourished anyway, as did most of the other children in Dadaab; all ending up with the refugee look of large stomachs, thin legs and sad eyes.

On the way to the UN Center, I passed hundreds of huts, with children playing outside in the sand, some wearing t-shirts, but most were bare naked. The appearance of malnutrition was the norm. I saw hopelessness on the faces of their parents, mostly mothers, as fathers would be away fighting in the war or trying to make some money in the city. It was the look of hopelessness in the mothers' eyes, and the sadness in the children's eyes, that haunts me to this day. Everyone, including myself, had been uprooted from their homes, where life was well set up, even if you were dirt poor.

For us refugees, home was now living in tent city on a vast flat plain, with no animals, very little clothing, no work and no purpose. The turbulence in our country seemed to only be getting worse, with no hope of a centralized government to pull the country together. Within Dadaab, to find some semblance of normalcy, order, and protection, many of the people began to gather together amongst their own tribes and clans, just like what was happening in greater Somalia, where the country was falling back into tribalism.

I was in Dadaab for three years. Sadly, I consider that time a step up from village life, as well as a step in the direction to improve my living conditions. I didn't know whether I would get ever out of Dadaab, or if I would spend my life there, as many have done and are still doing.

I tell people that it was faith that got me out of my grandmother's village, out of Somalia, and out of the Dadaab. Usually, they ask, "How did faith get you out?" Sometimes we don't have plans, but suddenly an opportunity arises and we make the best out of it. When something like that takes place, completely out of your control, and your life changes entirely, that is a result of faith. Challenges force us to cry out and ask for help, which often increases our faith when we do receive assistance.

My chance of leaving Dadaab was very slim, maybe one in one hundred and fifty thousand. The population of Dadaab was increasing every single day. Out of thousands and thousands of people who needed help, why was I picked? I can only say that, for all of us, there's a bigger plan that we're usually unaware of, but we need to be ready when those opportunities are presented to us. When we are given opportunities, we have an obligation to give it our best effort out of appreciation.

Chapter 10

WINNING THE LOTTERY

L ate in the summer of 1998, my cousin Hawo said to me, "Habibo, we need to apply to go to America. It is time to leave this camp." So, we applied. My mother applied for her and my siblings. Hawo and I applied together, as I was living with her at the time, helping with her kids. She had six kids under the age of seven and her husband was not there to assist. We submitted the paperwork by July, along with thousands of others who had the same hopes like us. We forgot about the application and went back to our daily routines. We didn't think we had a good chance at being selected.

Each day, we checked the UN center to see if the list of those selected to immigrate to America had been posted. They would post it inside a gated area, taping it to an open door. Every day, people would look for their ID number to see if it were on the paper. If your ID number was posted, that meant you've been picked for processing. If your ID was not there, then you could try again, for as many years as you cared to apply. I imagine there are people to this day who are still trying! Several weeks after we applied, Hawo went to see if the list was posted. Normally, it was posted by Thursday or Friday.

It was Thursday afternoon, a day I will never forget. I was staying with Hawo's children; three were napping and three were playing outside. Hawo went to the center to see if we had been selected; she always felt sure we would be chosen. I had my doubts. Out of thousands of people, why would we be selected?

I was sitting outside her tent, watching her youngest son play in the sand, when suddenly, Hawo came screaming back to the tent. She was ecstatic, jumping up and down and screaming. She was happier than I'd ever seen her. "Habibo, we are selected! We are selected!"

I was shocked. I said, "Selected? Are you sure?"

"Yes! We are selected, Habibo. We're going to United States of America, the land of opportunities."

No one could be that excited and filled with joy and not mean what they were saying. It hit me. I started screaming and jumping up and down with her. We were crying and hugging each other. We were so happy. Then, I remembered my mother. I told Hawo that I wanted to go and inform my mom. I ran off towards our tent. I didn't know how she was going to take the news. Here I was, a young single girl with no relatives or friends in America. I had to help her take care of my siblings. I didn't know if she'd let me out of that commitment. I thought to myself, "I want to go. I need to go to America, make lots of money and get out of this shit hole!" I ran as fast as I could to our camp – jubilant and giddy with happiness.

My mother was sitting outside our tent, holding Mohamed and watching the other kids play with the neighbors in the sand. I ran up to her and said, "Mom, guess what! We won! Hawo and I won the lottery! "

My mom, trying to make sense out of it, said, "What are you talking about? To America? Habibo, settle down and tell me." I could barely speak, "We won the lottery! Can I go? I want to go. I want to work, so I can help you. I want to send you money."

My mom answered, "You know what, Habibo? Sure, why not? I trust you. You need to go to America."

I was so happy. I had won the jackpot. It's a feeling I will never forget.

This was the first time I thought about the reality of going to America. We filled out the paperwork to go to America, and submitted it just like everyone else, like it was part of our routine. I had no clue that it would happen. I was surprised by my mother's encouragement. She told me that it was time for me to do more with my life, to try and make something of myself. She said there were many opportunities in America and that I was a smart girl.

"Habibo, you can do this. You can make a better life for yourself." My mother said

Unfortunately, my mother and my siblings weren't selected and never were. She was excited for me. This is where I've seen greatness in my mother. I've seen it in her strength. This is why I love her so much.

A week or so later, notices posted at the UN center told us the first part of the process was to begin. A date was set for everyone who had been selected to go to the center and begin the process. We were filled with anticipation; however, the anxiety of the unknown began creeping in. I realized I was going to a new country by myself. I didn't know if I had the skills to make it in America. All I knew was how to herd animals and take care of my siblings.

We went to the center on the appointed day and waited in a long line. Everyone in the line was happy and excited, like new life was breathed into them. It took the whole day because there were lots of people. We stood all morning as the line moved slowly. At high noon, the UN workers took their two-hour lunch break while everyone remained standing in line. Fortunately, we were told to bring food and water with us because once we got into the gate, we weren't allowed to leave until after being processed.

The volunteers took fingerprints and pictures, wrote down our information, and then let us go. The next day, we were told to go back so they could ask more questions. One of the lady volunteers asked me, "Why do you want to go to the United States?"

I responded, "I want to work, go to school and help my mom."

She asked me, "Have you ever been to school?

"No, I could never afford that." I told her

She then asked me, "Habibo, have you ever been afraid? Have you ever seen anything horrifying or bad?"

Her question hit me like a brick wall. I broke down crying right in front of her. Here was this total stranger, talking to me like no one had ever talked to me before. No one had ever asked about my feelings or incidents that had shaped my life. She wanted to know if I had experienced anything that was distressing.

I said, "Yes, I have. I have seen people get brutally killed. I have seen women raped in front of me." I told her about the abuse by older relatives and fending off the camel boy, successfully and unsuccessfully, while out living as a nomad. I told her about the things I saw during the civil war in 1993.

I talked about the desperate state my mom and siblings were in because we were so poor. The woman's question triggered a whole flood of feelings and frustrations within me. I told her everything. She looked me right into my eyes, and said, "Habibo, I am going to do everything in my power to make sure that you live the life you dream of. I will make sure that you get an education and that someday you feel safe." "Thank you, thank you so much," I told her, and I meant it from the bottom of my heart.

Two of my best friends who lived near our camp went through the same process, but after being selected and interviewed, they failed the interview and were found ineligible to go. They were angry at me. Their father even said to my mom, "You cannot send your daughter. She's just a teenager and too young. You don't want her to go over there. She's going to turn into a Christian and I would not advise you to let her go."

My mother answered, "Listen, I trust my daughter. She's very smart and I'm going to let her go."

I passed my interview, so did my cousin, Hawo; we were unbelievably emotional. A couple weeks later, a posting at the UN Center told us we would be leaving Dadaab in one week, never to return. We would take a bus and go to Nairobi, where we would get our medical examinations done. It was at that moment that the reality sank in. I was going away to another place that I didn't know of, and I wouldn't be coming back. I would be leaving my little brother and sisters, my mother, the village, my grandmother and uncles – all of them!

I had no idea what to expect in America. I didn't know what was going to happen to me, but I made a commitment to work hard and give us a better life. I knew I was going to give my best. We didn't have TVs, computers, magazines, or newspapers to show us what America was like. We heard that the country was full of money and riches; that people were wealthy beyond imagination and that it was available to all. I thought there would be money everywhere, just flowing from windows. There were times I felt sad and afraid, but I had to be brave.

Before leaving Dadaab, those who were going to America had to gather at a guarded fence in the area. It was a piece of open land with a few trees, like what you'd see livestock kept in. Hawo, her family and I, along with the others, were kept in that gated area. We were ready to go when the buses came the next day; they wanted to avoid any mistakes or mix-ups with people who hadn't been approved trying to leave.

It felt odd to be locked in, but no one cared; we were so anxious and happy to have been chosen for a new life. I remember the day like it was yesterday. It was hot and sticky with very little shade. We had water, but nowhere to go to the bathroom. If you had to relieve yourself, you did so over by the fence, with no privacy. It was demeaning, going to the bathroom in front of everybody, but what else could we do? Put up a fuss? Demand better conditions? We just went along with it.

As night fell, we had to sleep there, curled up on the ground. We were waiting for the night to pass, the sun to rise and the buses to come and take us away. We knew what we were getting into, but it wasn't very pleasant. We were willing to do anything to come to America! I was used to sleeping on the ground, so it wasn't a new experience for me. For those people from the cities, I could tell, it was difficult. At least there was a locked fence, which, for once, allowed us to sleep without fear of being robbed and raped.

Early in the morning, shortly after sunrise, the UN volunteers returned to the camp with several large buses. They woke us up, unlocked the gate and had us get on to the buses. It was exciting when things started to move; we all knew that the universe had smiled on us and we were off to a new life.

The ride to Nairobi was long, and it took all day. We rode across Kenya, raising all kinds of dust behind us with the bus. It was crowded. I had time to look out the window, to think about my life and the strange turn of events that were occurring. I realized I wouldn't be seeing this landscape for quite some time or ever again. I thought a lot about my grandmother, Ahmed and my life in the village. I thought about the crocodiles. I remembered hiding in the woods at night, away from neighboring tribes trying to invade our village. I remembered the bouts I had with malaria. I thought about the worst time of my life, being out on my own with the cows as a nomad. It seemed like it all happened such a long time ago.

We finally arrived in Nairobi at nightfall and we were taken to an area of the city called Iselee. Here in America, you'd call it a ghetto or slum. It was, and still is, a place, full of garbage everywhere in the streets. It was raining when we got there, making it all the worse. The place was filled with homeless children, drug addicts and alcoholics. Many people were sleeping right in the streets. The muddy streets had the foulest smell you could ever imagine. Your leg would sink into the mud, almost to your knee, and if you didn't pull your clothing up, it got covered with mud and human waste.

Each day, we had to take the bus to downtown Nairobi for our medical checkups. We were gone all day, waiting in lines, having vitals taken, various blood, stool and urine tests, dental exams, x-rays, and vaccinations. I had never had a vaccination; I didn't even know what they were. Start to finish, it took a week to complete all the medical exams.

The following week, we had orientation. Each day, we took a bus three hours out of Nairobi, to a center set up to prepare refugees for their transition to new countries. We would leave at 5 o'clock in the morning and wouldn't return until 6 or 7 o'clock at night. They explained all sorts of things to us in a classroom setting: the American legal system, Basic English phrases like, "Where is the restroom?", "Thank you", "Please", "What time is it?", "Where am I?"

We were told what to do and what not to do so we can fit in the western world. We were told not to start fights or pick arguments with people. We were told to be careful in the inner cities and to mind our own business. And we were told about the 911 system. There was a big misconception among us about calling 911; a lot of the kids were saying, "I can call 911 if my parents yell at me because the police will come and protect me." The parents were thinking, "Oh my God, I am not going to America because my kids will call 911 on us." It's funny, looking back at it now. We were taught what to expect when we first arrived in America, describing the various states we'd be going to, the weather, and how to be prepared. They gave us a book about all these different things. I didn't speak any English, nor could I read, so I just left my book in Nairobi.

Each day, my routine consisted of checking the lists that were posted to see when my flight would be leaving. Day after day, other names would appear, but not mine. Finally, around the first week of August, I went to see if my name was on the list, and sure enough, there it was. I was going to leave on the 27th of August. I got so excited and nervous, almost sick to my stomach with anxiety – the time had come to leave Africa and go to America!

When my mother found out I was leaving, she brought my brother and sisters to Nairobi so we could spend some time together. They stayed with my stepdad's sister, who lived in Nairobi. While waiting for my flight, I went and helped my mom with the kids. I saw how hard she was struggling, with no money and without help with the kids. One time, she made some porridge out of corn, and we didn't have anything to eat it with – no milk, no soup, or anything. I realized then, I had to go to America, so I could get my mother and my siblings out of there and help them out.

As the day approached for me to leave, other people were going shopping, buying clothes, and getting all excited to go to America. I didn't have any money to buy clothes, but I did have a skirt, a blouse and a long dress with two or three kamaars (head coverings). I had two gifts from different people and a small piece of luggage that one of my distant aunts lent me. I had an ear ring that my mom bought me, and I gave it back to her saying, "Mom you keep this. I am going to America and I can buy one there. You keep this, you need it more than I do."

The day we left was a sad one. I wouldn't be seeing my mother or my siblings for quite some time. The flight was scheduled to leave at eight o'clock at night, but I had to be there at 5 o'clock to be processed and secured inside a gated area again. I had become used to being put inside a gated area; it reminded me of my animals that had to go into their corral each night so they wouldn't wander off. That whole day, I was so nervous. I couldn't eat, I had diarrhea, and I couldn't sleep. I was a mess, but I was showing a brave face. The UN volunteers came to take us to the airport; it was time to leave. I kissed my mother and my sibling's goodbye. I hugged them for a long time. I knew I wouldn't be feeling their arms around my neck for quite a while. I got into the van with two other families, waved goodbye and didn't look back. It was a sad scene, but I didn't want to cry. I wanted to be strong for them. I wanted to provide them with a better life. My mom said to me, "Habibo, be strong and stay positive. Trust yourself,

you will meet nice people and somehow you will find
a way."

Chapter 11

WHERE IS AMERICA?

Our plane left the Nairobi airport at 8 in the afternoon – destination: Amsterdam. It is a city I had never heard of. I couldn't imagine where it was or what it looked like. Little did I know, it's one of the centers of the western world. It's also where most international flights arrive and depart from. I noticed how large the plane was; I couldn't imagine how it would get off the ground. It was so much bigger than the little cargo plane I took from Beledwayne to Nairobi three years earlier. It had three seats across, then the aisle and three more seats across – and seatbelts! It takes riding in a cargo plane on burlap bags of khat, worrying about being tossed across the floor from the turbulence, to appreciate the seats in a regular commercial airplane.

When I got settled into my seat, it hit me hard that I was going to another world; an unknown world with people I didn't know. I didn't even know the language! I left my family, friends, animals, and the only life I had ever known. No more swimming in the river or grazing the animals out on the grasslands. No more fearing for my life or having to fight off camel boys. No more listening to the criticism of my uncle, Abdi, or the harshness of my grandmother. I was leaving my sibling whom I bonded with in the last three years. I was practically their mother. With all that, I started to panic. I wanted to get off the plane and go back to my grandmother's village, even though that was exactly what I was praying to leave. I thought, "What am I getting myself into?" The plane doors were closed and locked, and we were already on the runway ready to take off - there was no turning back now! I thought, "America, here I come."

I was so emotional; excited, scared, nervous, anxious, all at the same time. At times, I felt numb, like I was in a dream. The plane was full of other Somalis – many were refugees and some were just flying out of Nairobi. I started feeling feverish with a dry hacking cough. We arrived in Amsterdam at 10 o'clock in the morning. The UN workers were at the gate, waiting to help refugees as we got off the plane. There were several of them smiling and holding up welcome signs. Each person took twenty of us to the cafeteria to eat. I didn't recognize any of the food and I had no idea what to get. I had never seen hamburger, fries, or hot dogs. What's Coke, Sprite, or Pepsi? What on the earth is Ketchup? I got an orange drink, whereas I could have had whatever I wanted. We only had to wait three hours in Amsterdam for our flight to New York. In less than twenty-four hours, I was leaving the second continent

I had ever been to and we were off to a third one – North America!   We left at 11 o'clock at night. I was getting sicker, at a time when I should have been feeling my best. I could barely walk, I had a terrible headache, and I was vomiting. I was nervous.

I had experienced a lot in my life, but flying by myself to a strange land with no one there to pick me up at the airport or help me find my way in the United States, was extremely stressful. What gave me courage was the thought that I had to do it for my mother and my siblings. It gave me a purpose and a job to do – that's the only thing that kept me going. If it weren't for that, I don't think I could've done it. Somehow, when we do things for others, especially things that are difficult or fearsome, we gather courage, whereas, if we do it for ourselves, it seems much harder.

Finally, when I didn't think I could sit in my seat any longer, the pilot announced that we were approaching New York City.   I looked out the window and I was astonished. I had never seen so much bright lights in my life; the whole sky, and as far as I could see, was filled with lights. Lights were shining so bright and reflecting off the water, the whole sky lit up as if it was filled with diamonds and jewels. It was the most beautiful sight I had ever seen in my life!   The sky scrapers!   I couldn't believe buildings could be made so tall. I thought, "America truly is a rich country." In the village and in Dadaab, there were no lights, not even electricity. There was nothing but huts.

From the airport, we took a bus to our hotel. I remember crossing a bridge and looking out over the water at the New York skyline. It was breathtaking. I knew I was a long way from the grasslands of Somalia. It was a long bus ride to the hotel; it seemed like it took hours and hours. The hotel we were brought to, was beautiful – it had sheets and blankets and pillows, and it smelled great. I had never seen soap, shampoo and conditioner, much less, little bottles of them. I had never seen such luxury before - and the pillows! For someone that never slept with a pillow, that was the ultimate! There were even extra pillows and blankets in the closets. Four of us stayed in the hotel room together, three other women and myself. I was the youngest of them all.

It's hard to imagine how this all appeared to us. It felt like we were saved. It was a humbling experience. I thought, "Why me? How do I deserve this? What sort of kindness is this, to bring us this long way and help us?"

We woke up in the morning to one of the women saying, "Let's go. We have to go. Hurry up." We got up and didn't even have time to clean up. I quickly washed my face and brushed my teeth, a little bewildered over the toothpaste and toothbrush, as I had never used either before. In Somalia, we use a brush made from the branches of the Roomay tree, rubbed against our teeth. I thought the tooth paste was disgusting, foaming and frothing in my mouth. I am used to it now, but the first time was an odd experience. I still finish my teeth with a Roomay tree stick – it's very refreshing. I wore the same clothes I left home in, with nothing else to change into, and rushed out of the hotel room.

We were shown to the hotel breakfast area. I had juice and a sweet roll. I had never seen anything like that before, but it was good. Quickly after breakfast, we were off to the airport to catch a plane to Dallas. Only a certain number of us were to go to Dallas and on to Phoenix, while others were distributed to different parts of the country. Some refugees went to Virginia, Nebraska, Ohio, California, North Carolina, or Minnesota.

We waited in the gated area for our flight. We were quite a sight, all dressed in our Somali garbs and head coverings, none of us speaking the language, constantly looking lost. This time, I was ready for the plane ride. I wanted a window seat, so I could see this land called America. We flew during the daytime, which was great, and I had a chance to look out over the countryside. It was pretty! I could see the lakes and rivers, fields of different crops, small towns and cities way below us. It seemed so orderly, with roads crisscrossing the country side, and fields of crops laid out in patterns. It was a wonderful feeling for a young girl. As we were about to land, we flew above Dallas. Looking out over the city, I thought, "So, this is America!"

From Dallas, we took another plane to Phoenix, which was a short ride. When we landed, social workers met us there, holding up signs with our names written on them. I thought it was so funny that they'd do that; it worked, though.

The social worker took three of us, me and two older women, to an apartment where we were to live. First, he took us to a food store in Phoenix to buy some supplies. He brought us into the grocery store, and we just stood there like a deer in headlights. None of us had ever seen such a thing. We were used to buying food in small open markets, at best. Here, the market was huge and inside a building, with more food and supplies than I've ever seen before. To us it was opulent, wealth beyond belief, with so much food and so many choices. We had no idea what to buy. Our social worker told us to go and get whatever we wanted. He didn't realize that we didn't even know where to start or what to look for. We were in a major cultural shock; hardly able to move or look around the store.

I bought a large carrot cake and some orange juice. Can you believe it? A carrot cake! To this day, every time carrot cake is served, I laugh inside, remembering my first choice of food. One of the other women picked a big bag of oranges. The social worker spoke in Arabic, which I somewhat understood. He said, "Is that all you're going to get?" I told him I didn't know what to get. He said, "OK." He paid for the food and we left.

Looking back, there were other things that would have been better for me than carrot cake, such as fruit, chicken, milk or bread. The social worker was expecting us to stock up for our apartment. I believe he was in a culture shock, as well. We were completely out of our element and we didn't know how to get what we needed. The store completely blew us away. It would have been nice for the man to guide us through and help us pick out some things. However, I still like carrot cake!

He brought us to the apartment we were to live in. It was a one bedroom apartment on the second floor. It had two twin mattresses with box springs on the floor; each bed had a pillow, sheets and a few blankets. Each of us was given soap, a toothbrush, toothpaste, a cup, a plate, eating utensils, and three cooking pots. The first evening in the apartment, I went to bed early, having had very little sleep. I still wasn't feeling well and I was completely overwhelmed.

The other women were older than me, in their late twenties. They were from the same tribe and I was from an opposite tribe that was fighting against theirs. Our tribe had beaten theirs during the civil war and they were upset with me. They rejected me instantly, and wouldn't have anything to do with me. It was tense and uncomfortable.

The social worker came by in the morning to take us to the Social Security office, where we did our paperwork. From there, we went to the social services agency to receive $200 each in food stamps and "Welcome to America" cash amount of $150, a one-time thing. When we got back to the apartment, I was dead sick. I couldn't swallow, I had a rash, my eyes were burning, and my throat was sore. For two days, I laid in my bed, so sick I could barely get up to go to the bathroom. To make matters worse, the ladies were mean. They told me I was not good enough or smart enough because I was from the country. They would make their food and tea, and then throw out what was left over; never offering me anything because of our tribal differences. I don't know which was worse, being sick to death or being ignored and humiliated by my roommates. They called me derogatory names and bullied me. What a way to start my stay in America. It's not what I expected, but, I was used to the tribal differences that had been prevalent in the refugee camp. There, we would avoid each other, but here, we had no choice. The social workers didn't know about tribes and the trouble occurring in Somalia.

After a few days, a kind social worker came by. It was a Tuesday. She asked my roommates where I was – "the third person". They said, "Oh, she's in bed. We don't know what's wrong with her." The social worker came in and touched my forehead. Right away she said, "Come on. We're going to the hospital."

I crawled out of my bed, feeling dizzy and lightheaded. I got dressed, and she held my arm as she took me to the hospital in Phoenix. I was admitted in, and they gave me fluids, took blood sample, and gave me some IV medications. The social worker stayed with me the whole time; she was a wonderful woman. She was the first person I had any meaningful contact with. I wish I could see her again and thank her, but I don't know her name. I don't think I would have made it without her. It shows that with help, you can do anything. If she ever happens to read this book, I truly hope she contacts me so I can thank her.

I was in the hospital for all day and night before I went back to the apartment. The girls were even more malicious now. They'd make common jokes about me and talked about how they hated my tribe. They would say that I shouldn't even be in America – I didn't deserve it. I was used to insults and criticism. I didn't like it, but I could take it.

One day, we took a bus to downtown. At one bus stop, they got off at the back of the bus and ditched me. The bus took off and I had no idea where we were going or where to get off. I couldn't read any English or any of the street signs. I finally got off and sat on the bus bench, not knowing what to do. Providentially, a Somali man came by and asked what I was doing. I told him what had happened, and that I had no idea where I was or how to get home. He told me there was only one bus and that I should take it and get off at a certain street. I did what he told me and found my way back to the apartment.

I was in the apartment with these women for about a month. Several Somali males would come by to visit us. Men heard there were some women living together, who were new to America. The men were looking for mates. One of them, Aden, visited often. He had a car and would help us by giving us rides. He helped us fill out job applications. A friend of his worked at the Ritz Carlton hotel and he helped two of us girls get jobs there. If it weren't for him and other immigrants, who understood our predicament, we would have had a challenging time. They showed us what we needed to do.

One act of kindness that I'll never forget, happened at the Ritz Carlton on my first day at work. I had my one pair of sandals, brought with me from Dadaab, so that's what I wore to work. The supervisor, Emilio, a nice, young Mexican man, told me I couldn't wear sandals at work, and that I needed regular shoes. I told him I didn't have regular shoes and I didn't have money to buy a pair. He went to his locker and brought me a pair of his shoes, they were black dress shoes. I was so impressed that a man was kind enough to give me his shoes. I thanked him, and wore his shoes every day, until I could afford to buy my own. I wonder how many American girls would wear a pair of men's black dress shoes to work each day for a month - probably not too many! I thought it was great.

For my first job at the Ritz Carlton, I started working as a dishwasher in the kitchen. At first, it was overwhelming. It was hard getting used to the work schedule; starting at a certain time every day, breaks at another time, with time clocks. That kind of work was new to me. The dishes just kept coming. I had never used machines before; spraying water, running the dishes through the washer, and re-stacking them once they were cleaned.

The new life as a dishwasher was all a blur to me. I didn't even know how to tell the time. I had to learn quickly. One of the guys at the Carlton who liked me taught me how to read the clock. I had seen watches before I have never seen clocks on walls, where everyone watched them all day long. In the village, we would tell time by the shadows cast from the sun. We could tell whether it was midday or time to start heading home.

One difficult thing about working for the hotel was that we weren't allowed to wear a scarf or dresses - only pants and a blouse. What a shock! There were several Somali women who refused work because of this. I felt like I had no choice. I had to do what I had to do – good lessons learned from Grandma in the village! What helped me was remembering my mother and siblings back in their tent at Dadaab, trying to barter for powdered milk or tea. I put on my pants and shirt, took the scarf off my head and went to work!

I felt like I was naked, wearing the navy-blue pants and my white shirt tucked in, with no scarf on my head! The first time I got my uniform, they asked me what size I wore. I said, "I don't know. What's a size?" I didn't even know what a "size" meant.

It took me one month after I started working to begin sending money to my mother. Usually it was $100, but sometimes as much as $300 per month – every month! I found out many Somali immigrants work two jobs, one for themselves and their family and one for their relatives back in their home country. As time went on, I sent $800, so my mother could rent a house in South Cea, a suburb of Nairobi. By continuing to send money, I helped her keep the house which she still lives in today. I have also sent enough money to put all my siblings through school.

It took me a very long time to get used to the food in America. There was food everywhere, especially at the Ritz Carlton – cookies, sweets, pastries, small sandwiches, large buffets, and I could eat there for free. I went from porridge and milk to more food than I have seen before. Pizza was the most amazing thing I ever tasted, I was mesmerized by it. McDonald's blew my mind. The day I went to McDonalds was the day I fell in love with America. Slowly, I got used to the culture here. I had to learn to drive, which was difficult. I also had to study English, so I went to an "English as a second language" class and I failed it!

One day at the Ritz Carlton hotel, an odd thing happened to me. A famous guest came to stay at the hotel, and he found out that there were Somali refugees working in the kitchen. He had the management bring him back to the kitchen. I was working, and saw there was a lot of fuss over this man. I realized he must have been someone important. He came into the kitchen and greeted us, hugging several of us, including myself. He asked to have his picture taken with me. Why me, I don't know, but I guess we connected. I had no idea who this man was. After the picture was taken, and the man left, I asked, "Who was that?" The guys in the kitchen broke out laughing, and said, "you are silly, girl, that was Mohammed Ali!"

Chapter 12

CONQUERING THE ODDS

"Your past does not equal your future." – Tony Robbins

"Nothing has any power over me other than that which I give it through my conscious thoughts." – Tony Robbins

"Your life changes the moment you make a new, congruent, and committed decision." - Tony Robbins

"Quality questions create a quality life." – Tony Robbins
"Questions provide the key to unlocking our unlimited potential." – Tony Robbins

---

I am glad I didn't arrive in a snowy area when first I came to America. Phoenix, Arizona is more like what I was accustomed to in Somalia and Kenya; hot and dry. I didn't have a lot to get used to with regards to the weather and climate. Why didn't anyone tell me about Minnesota? My first winter was terrible. I had never seen snow before; much less mountains of it with freezing, driving winds that take your breath away, freeze your face and almost knock you off your feet. And driving in it? Forget it! That was an adjustment for me. I would not be surprised if you saw some Somalis, especially ladies, wearing sandals when it's in the single digits outside. We are not used to wearing tennis shoes, much less boots.

My cousin, who asked me to move to Minnesota, forgot to mention she was not living alone, and that she did not have her own apartment. She was living with her friend, the friend's husband and their daughter in a two-bedroom apartment. My cousin, the little girl and I shared a bedroom, while the married couple slept in the other room. There were two twin beds in our room; the little girl slept in one, while my cousin and I slept in the other. I had to remind myself that this was not as bad as when I used to sleep on the ground and tie cloths around my feet to keep the worms from burrowing in, or a rope around my legs to prevent getting raped. After all, sleeping in a twin bed with a cousin was like heaven - we each had a pillow, and the sheets and blankets were clean.

Soon after I arrived, I became homeless. The little girl was spoiled; she would hit, pee, and bite you when she did not get her way. One morning, the little girl came over to our bed and started to jump up and down. I was tired. I worked two jobs and hadn't slept that night because I was on the phone with my mother and siblings back home. I asked the little girl to leave me alone.

"If you don't leave me alone, I will take your Barbie doll away." She screamed, pissed on herself and ran to her mother. She told her mother that I hit her and took her toy away. Suddenly, the mother walked into the room and told me to leave her house. She said, "You cannot stay here anymore. I do not like you and I do not like that you made my daughter cry." Suddenly, I was homeless.

The only phone number I had was Abdi's. I met him few weeks prior through my cousin. He took me out and showed me around. I remembered him giving me his telephone number in case I need anything. I called him and told him that I did not have place to stay. He called his sister and she said I could stay with her and her family. I was so thankful that he did that for me. I was comfortable at her house and she was a nice lady, but I wanted to have my own home. When Abdi said that he was interested in getting married to me, I did not hesitate. I knew deep down in my heart, I was not ready for marriage, but that is all I knew. When you hit puberty, you get married and have babies. He called my dad and uncle. In our culture, the man must talk to the girl's parents and get approval from them. I thought Abdi was going to chicken out, but he didn't. Within three months, we got married. I moved in with him into his small studio apartment. I finally had a home. When I was back in the village, dreaming about my own husband and hut, I had no idea it would be in Minneapolis, Minnesota. I didn't know what I was getting into. The idea of getting married and being married are completely different. I would not want my daughters or my son to get married at a young age.

I got pregnant right away with my oldest daughter, Najma. I continued to work and raised Najma, and then Nawal came two years later. If you have more than one child, did you wonder how you could love more than one child? Well, I did and I was terrified. I did not know how I would love two different people. I was not good at the whole "love thing". I was afraid to express affection to my child because I thought it was somehow dirty, or abnormal. I would ask myself, "Why am I feeling this way? I have two amazingly adorable girls so I needed to get my head and heart to align." Deep down, I knew I loved my girls. They meant the world to me, but why was it so hard for me to expressive my love for them? I couldn't I say the words "I love you" out loud! What was my problem?

> *"Sometimes, when you pick up your child, you can feel the map of your own bones beneath your hands, or smell the scent of your skin in the nape of his neck. This is the most extraordinary thing about motherhood – finding a piece of yourself separate and apart that all the same you could not live without."* — Jodi Picoult

One evening in early 2005, I was sitting with my two daughters in our tiny apartment in the public housing in St. Paul, Minnesota. It was late in the afternoon. Suddenly, I experienced an awakening. I could see the future for my children. The truth was, I was not setting a good example for my girls. I was living in public housing, where fights occurred every day. We had cockroaches and rats, paint peeling and a carpet that has never been changed. Until that moment, I thought my life was perfect. I was in America; my kids were safe and we had a roof over our heads. That late afternoon, something shifted in my soul. I was moved to my core.

> *"A real decision is measured by the fact that you've taken a new action. If there's no action, you haven't truly decided."*
> *– Tony Robbins*

I could not move; my limbs went numb and I sat there day dreaming about the possibilities. The possibilities I had never seen before. I thought to myself, "I need to go to school." How can I go to school, when I have never been to school before? Right then and there, I decided I was going to go to school no matter what. I will start from the bottom and get to the top. I will not ever give up. I will crawl if I must.

Now that I am older and wiser, I realized I was practicing the law of attraction: Speak what you want, as if you already have it. Not "maybe", not "if", but speak with precision and conviction. According to David J Schwartz, our mind is a thought factory. It is busy producing positive and negative thoughts. The key is to utilize your positive thoughts and minimize the negative thoughts. You can acknowledge the negative thoughts, but you do not have to live there. As he said in The Magic of Thinking Big, "Use Mr. Triumph 100 percent of the time and when any thoughts enter in your mind ask Mr. Triumph to get to work; he will show up and you will succeed."

The next morning, I woke up early and asked my neighbor to watch the girls. I went to school to sign up for classes. They told me I needed to take a placement test for classes. I was anxious, sweaty, and excited at the same time. I will be the first to go to college in my family! I am going to do this for Najma and Nawal. I must do this for my girls. "This is my time". I was murmuring to myself the whole morning. The blonde lady at the reception desk asked me if something was wrong. I said, "No ma'am." She gave me a slight smile, and I continued with my incantation.

I learnt that I should work for whatever I wanted! I launched my endeavor to become a nurse. I decided to become an LPN to improve my working situation and my salary, and then I would go on to become an RN. I took all my prerequisites such as anatomy, chemistry, math and English and ended up with a 4.0 grade point average. When I was applying to the LPN program at the community college, my school friends said, "Habibo, you will not survive this school. They are tough and racist. They will make you fail."

I told them, "If my hard work and good attitude do not get me through this school, then I have worked for nothing. I have good work ethics and dedication; I have never backed out of a challenge and I'm not going to quit now." To my surprise, I was accepted into the LPN program. I was so excited. I couldn't believe it happened.

At first, the other students and teachers treated me like I was a second-class citizen. They shied away from me. I even had teachers say to me, "Habibo, nursing is going to be too hard for you.

Why don't you think about doing something else? You're more suited to wash dishes or clean houses." This kind of talk only fuels my determination. Those students and teachers didn't know it, but they did me a favor. I had set my mind to accomplishing this task, and I was going to do it.

After the first term, I maintained a 4.0 grade point average. Immediately, all the poor treatment and snide remarks stopped. I had students asking to study with me, and teachers treating me with respect. Is there a lesson here? It's sad that one must be great to be liked. What about those who don't do so well?

"It's not over until you win" - Les Brown

At our graduation, I'll never forget the speech given by one of our instructors. I thought this instructor was the most difficult to get along with. During her speech for the graduating class, she said, "There is one student who was the quietest, the most dedicated and the most likely to succeed – Habibo!" I was shocked; I didn't know what to think, but I was very happy for the praise, as I worked hard.

Chapter 13

SEEING MY MOTHER AGAIN

When was the last time you have seen your mother? Yesterday, last week, last month, last year? How often do you talk to her? Most people who come to America including myself had to give up something to be here and make a new life. One of the hardest thing is giving up the ability to see and be with our family. When my friends complain about their parents or family members over involving in their life, I smile and tell them to enjoy what they have because the grass is not always greener on the other side. I wish I could see my mother more often than once in seventeen years.

Since I moved my mother and siblings out of Dadaab, they have lived in Nairobi. The kids have gone to school there, and are doing well. I miss my mom and my siblings more than anything. Not seeing them for twelve years was extremely hard.

When I first came to the United States back in 1999, I filed a sponsorship for my mother and my siblings. I worked hard to bring them here, but it didn't work out the way I was hoping. When I first filed the papers, my mother got a letter a year after stating she would be contacted for a formal interview. It took two more years before she got that interview. She and the rest of the family had to go through a primary interview, secondary interview, and were finally told they passed all the processing and could expect their orientation times within the next few months. They had their orientation, which informs you on things you need to know before you enter the United States. They completed orientation in May 2003. I was so excited, and was hoping that they would come before the birth of my second daughter who was due later that year.

I received a call from the office of Catholic Charities to sign the Affidavit of Support form for the family, which states that I would provide for their board and room the first six months. I was ecstatic to sign this paper, knowing that in a few weeks to a month, I would see my family again. We waited anxiously. The weeks turned into months, and months into years. During this waiting period, my mother and I had been writing and calling to find out what was the hold up, and if there was anything we could do to speed up the process. My hopes and dreams of reuniting with my family were shattered. I became sad, depressed and gave up all hope of them coming to the US.

My family had three medical checkups, six interviews, two orientations, a DNA test, but ultimately, in November of 2009, they were told that they were not accepted to the United States. Ten years of waiting and hoping; ten years our lives were on hold. I used to think those people do not have hearts, because as a human being, how can you do that to people - make them wait for ten years then tell them, "Sorry we cannot accept you"? It would be better if they had told us from the beginning, so that my family and I could move on with our lives, and we could plan to reunite in some other ways.

In early 2010, when I finally realized that my family was not coming to the United States, I made the decision to go and visit them in Kenya. This was not an easy decision, mainly due to the cost. My mother had not met any of my kids, and more than anything, she wanted to see her grandchildren. When I called my mother to inform her that I was going to visit, my mother's first reaction was, "Oh! Good! I am finally going to see my grandchildren."

I told her, "I am sorry to disappoint you Mom, but I can't bring the kids due to the cost."

She was very disappointed. It was hard not being able to take my kids with me, so they could see my family, but that was almost impossible. When I left, I kissed my children goodbye, got on the plane and headed back to Africa.

The plane landed in Nairobi early in the morning. Of course, no one was there to meet me. Why this always happens to me, I don't know, but I got used to it. Rather than panicking, I simply waited, knowing someone, sometime would show up. I decided to have some coffee, so I sat with a man in the coffee shop who was from Washington, DC. We had a good conversation, and I thought how odd it was that only a dozen years after I left Dadaab, barely old enough to be called an adult, not knowing any English, uncultured and rather ignorant about the world, here I was sitting and conversing about American politics with a man from the nation's capital.

As we were talking, I looked up and saw my mother and my uncle Ahmed, walking towards me. Ahmed, in his long flowing robe looked so stately, although he appeared much older and thinner with gray hair. His eyes were still soft and gentle. My mother also showed the years on her face, now having six children to take care of, all in their teenage years.

I jumped up and ran toward them. I first ran to my mother and hugged her for what seemed like forever, not wanting to let go. Then, I hugged Uncle Ahmed and we all started to cry with joy. I couldn't have wished for anyone else in the world to come there to greet me. They kept commenting on how I had become such a grown woman.

Ahmed said, "Habibo, the last time I saw you, you were a little girl. Now, you are a woman and a beautiful one."

I spent sixteen days with them in Nairobi. We did all the family things that people do: we slept, ate, shopped, and I spent time playing with the kids, getting to know each other. I had so much fun going out and shopping with them. I bought them new clothes, shoes, and little things they couldn't afford.

It was odd being back in Africa. Not much was different. The thing that had changed the most was me as my world view had changed. I was not so naïve anymore. I was able to think for myself and communicate as I wished. I actually had opinions.

My mother's apartment, which I helped to pay for several years before, was kind of a shock to me. It was in an old building, slightly crumbling and not very well kept. They lived on the first floor which got dirty quite easily. Most of the apartments had running water, but not hot water. Toilets were inside, but if the water is suddenly turned off, then it's impossible to flush. Sometimes the water is off for several days to a week.

I told my mother, "Mom, I am getting you out of here. I think we can find something much nicer for you." We looked around and found a nice apartment on the third floor of a different building. I paid for it and helped her move in with the kids.

When I left, I felt much better knowing that they were in good living conditions – safer, cleaner, and spacious.

I thought about the last time I saw my mother and siblings, living in a makeshift tent on the edge of Dadaab refugee camp, I felt proud to see them living more civilized with beds and sheets, towels and several sets of clothes. It made me feel good that I could help them have those comforts. I could see that all my efforts immigrating to the United States, and working as hard as I did for years, had its rewards. Not only for myself, but for them as well. It affirmed that what I was doing was worthwhile.

I looked back on everything that happened in my past, being a toddler in my grandmother's hut by myself, eating porridge and playing with mud, to the times my cousin would visit the hut or when I stayed with them, to all the times I went out with the animals into the grasslands. I thought about how rugged a person would have to be to do that, to work each day walking sheep, goats and cows for miles so they could eat, and then fighting off the wild animals trying to eat the herd. I remembered the crocodile that looked into my eyes – I'll never forget his! Trust me, you don't want to experience that. I thought about the times I was taken advantage of as a young girl and as I grew up, until I went to Dadaab, when it finally stopped, and I didn't have to fight anymore.

I looked out the plane window, as we were flying over the Atlantic. Here I was, dressed nicely, carrying a purse with money and charge cards, a U.S. citizen with a driver's license. I am a registered nurse, flying home to my job at the Mayo Clinic. I have a nice house with a large screen TV, furniture, king size bed with lots of pillows, and my children! I thought to myself, "What a life! How did I get here?"

"Patience, persistence and perspiration make an unbeatable combination for success." - Napoleon Hill

---

I am still processing what I went through in my life, especially the most difficult times. Surprisingly enough, it's not the times I had to fight the camel boys off or when I was treated badly by my fifteen-year-old cousin. It's the criticism and belittlement, and the lack of support and care that I had to endure growing up as a young girl. The feeling of being a farm hand, not being wanted, not belonging to anyone. That's the hard part! I didn't have hugs and kisses or people telling me they loved me. There was no praise of any kind. Being alone was hard!

I realize now that I wasn't the only one going through it. Thousands and thousands of people all over the world go through it, and not just in third world countries. Right here in America, I see it all around me in the faces and eyes of young girls and boys, as well as adults.

I am sharing my story with you, because it's so common to many people, especially many young girls around the world. Those girls who still live in my village, those young men and women who are still nomads who have never set feet in a school, who are not aware of their brilliant talents, who have never been told they are worth more than just bearing children. For those girls and boys who were born in Dadaab, who have no hope of getting out of there and, most importantly, no hope whatsoever for an education. I'm writing this for anyone whose innocence has been stolen as a child, for anyone who has been told they were not good enough, pretty enough or anyone who ever felt left out or unloved. This is for you!

When a child is born, he/she is innocent and deserves the absolute best, life can provide. Parents are responsible for   providing that child with support: financial, educational, spiritual, emotional, and an overall sense of well-being. One of the most important things I found out in my life is that a child needs to know he or she is being loved by his or her parents, unconditionally. The child needs to know that a parent's love cannot be bought or denied. The child does not need to earn it; he/she is rather entitled to it. With love and appreciation, children can develop a sense of belonging and can grow up to become self-sufficient, independent, successful individuals who can contribute to society. No child should ever feel unloved or unworthy of love.

"By making eye-contact, getting down to your child's level, offering a touch, or using a tone of your voice that conveys a desire to genuinely connect, you disarm yourself. You make it possible to reach your child more deeply and truly move forward together." – Hilary Flower

I am sharing my story because I want to make a difference, I want to advocate for young girls who have no opportunity for education. With education, we can eradicate ignorance. There are millions of children who have no access to schools in sub-Sahara Africa or Asia. Of those children, eighty percent are girls.

Sharing my story is one of the most difficult things I've had to do in my life, because it required revisiting certain aspects of my life that I buried a long time ago. Despite the difficulty, I've been very fortunate. God had plans for me, and He still does. My faith has grown much stronger as I see how life can turn out. Sometimes life throws us good things, as well as challenges. From each of these things, we learn.

People ask me, "Habibo, how were you able to do what you did?"

I say, "Plain and simple - sheer determination to survive, to improve, and to make a better life for myself and those around me."

I take no for answer. I refuse to give up. I refuse to be placed in a box.

I especially try to be for my children, the way no one had been for me. My attitude with them is not one of criticism – ever! When they try something and fail, I say, "Don't worry about it. You'll get it next time. Keep on practicing"

"You are an infinite spiritual being having a temporary human experience." – Wayne W. Dyer

---

I do not spoil my children either. I tell them that some people do not get the opportunities they have, many of which they need to work for and earn. I tell them to appreciate what they have, and I remind them of how I grew up. As a parent, I try to do the best I can, and as I get older, I realize new things every day. I also know I am far from being perfect.

Chapter 14

TURN YOUR VALLEY INTO A MOUNTAIN TOP

*"Commit to CANI! – Constant and Never-Ending
Improvement." – Tony Robbins*

Imagine being a prisoner of a troubled childhood? Image being emotionally crippled with the memory of war, starvation, beating and rape? Is it possible to bounce back from adversity and go on to live a healthy, happy and fulfilled life? Resilient people do not let adversity define them. They embrace adversity by moving towards their goal and beyond themselves, transcending pain and grief by perceiving challenges as ephemeral.

Sometimes it is easier to play the victim; I had to choose to build my resilience muscles. Each person has endured some hardships at a certain level in their life. It is up to us to decide whether we want to veg out in the pain and be stranded forever, or choose to bounce back from theses setbacks by resorting to persistence and resiliency. Persistence is the driving force behind success. In the face of problems and setbacks, it is the determination not to cave in or give. The ability to demonstrate resilience is paramount to a long-term success. One way to develop resilience is to cultivate an outlook of realistic optimism--that is, acknowledging current challenges while maintaining a hopeful perspective on the future.

"You are the only real obstacle in your path to a fulfilling life."
Les Brown

Focus on your mindset. There are lessons to be learned from every experience in life. Learning new things keeps you engaged, motivated, and helps you grow as an individual. It gives you a sense of accomplishment and boosts your self-confidence and resilience. Mental strength is necessary to help regulate emotions, manage thoughts, and behave positively. Despite our circumstances, we must understand how our thoughts dictate our behaviors and feelings. I have learned from Anthony Robbins that we must change our physiology to change our state of mind and emotions. For instance, if you are sitting and ruminating about a particular situation, get up quickly, increase your heart rate by walking fast or jumping jacks then shift your mind to the present moment and speak to yourself with self-affirmation whatever that might be for you. Interrupting your limiting beliefs and patterns release you and allow you to overcome your situation. You must replace your state of fear, pessimism or even anger with determination, gratitude, generosity, and curiosity.

"Wanting something is not enough. You must hunger for it. Your motivation must be absolutely compelling in order to overcome the obstacles that will invariably come your way."
—Les Brown

Adversity equals growth. Have you settled into a state of adversity? Have you allowed fear to dictate your current situations? Are you currently stuck? Well here are few key steps to help you take that leap of faith. The truth is that as long as you are breathing adversity big or small will knock on your door. Then the question is how do you respond when you go toe to toe with adversity. First: Do not panic and try to take control of the situation, and do not worry about what you cannot control. Focus on your own feelings, weigh your choices on how to react and feel. Stay positive, focusing on the goal to be achieved. Gain perspective by counting your blessings and remember that this particular adversity has been defeated by others before you. Seek help when needed. Find a mentor who can guide you. Do not change your goals, change your approach.

Resilience is built for the long haul, which can be achieved by discovering a mission and renewing the commitment to it, enjoying what you do, nurturing the will to win, finding control and coping with stress, and staying healthy. The capacity to bounce back from defeat leads to mental toughness, or resilience. Whenever you experience a disconnection between your desire and reality, it is a golden opportunity to build your resilience muscle. Success or failure in coping with setbacks has everything to do with how we choose to construe those setbacks. Resilience is not about being tough and hardcore. It consists of the following five steps:

-Stop and step back. This action allows people a degree of objectivity in their interpretations, a distance that allows for a bigger picture of challenges.

-Observe. It promotes objectivity.

-Ask Bigger Questions. Widening and deepening one's curiosity leads to bigger and more complex questions. The answers you get are the results of the types of questions you ask.

-Reword. It consists of reconfiguring a problem to see it as an opportunity. As Wayne Dyer said "If you change the way you look at things, the things you look at change."

One common way of reframing an adversity is to reflect upon how it might be a learning experience.

-Respond, don't react. Responding means following through with appropriate action; whereas reacting emanate more from habits with less thinking process.

Adversity can be viewed as a path to opportunity. The ability to bounce back from a setback; "resilience," is a characteristic of highly successful people.

"The strongest oak of the forest is not the one that is protected from the storm and hidden from the sun. It's the one that stands in the open where it is compelled to struggle for its existence against the winds and rains and the scorching sun."
— Napoleon Hill

Failure teaches people lessons and gives them the ability to be more resilient and move on. The traits of resilience, self-esteem, positivity, control, and confidence serve as the bridge between challenge and success in the world.

"If you don't like something, change it. If you can't change it, change your attitude." —Maya Angelou

---

The day we arrived at Amsterdam airport, I saw so many people, well dressed, looking sharp and walking at a fast pace. It depicted a dire contrast with my experiences in the village and at the refugee camp. Many thoughts flock to my mind and I knew at that moment I would do everything I can to become successful and help my family.

What is success and why do we need it? Success is getting all that you desire in life. It's finding fulfilment and your purpose in life. It's waking up in the morning feeling victorious rather than defeated. Being successful means the achievement of desired visions and planned goals. The feelings success brings will make you walk proudly in the streets with your head up high while being happy and satisfied. Many people dream of becoming successful but few reach success that brings fulfillment, joy and wealth. Why are so many people living in the same unhappy, unsuccessful, miserable life?

Growing up in Somalia as a nomad, I did not have to dream too big. My dreams between the age 4 and 13 was taking the cows, goats and sheep out to herd and bringing them back safely without missing one. And every day that I reached that goal, I was successful. My success and fulfilment were more limited to bringing the same number of herds back with no loss. I wished one day I would find a husband, build my own hut. Often times our success is limited by the environment we are in, people around us, and our limiting beliefs. You have to be out of the comfort zone to realize what success is.

* Think big: let your mind go wild into whatever you desire to achieve even though you do not know exactly what it is. Thinking big allows the mind to explore other realms. It makes you set higher, scarier goals that stretch your comfort zone. And as Michelangelo Buonarroti said, "The greater danger for most of us lies not in setting our aim too high and falling short; but in setting our aim too low, and achieving our mark."

*Find what comes easily to you that you are passionate about.

*Don't be scared to fail and restart. Every time you fail and restart, you are inventing yourself. Failing gives you the opportunity to find different and more efficient ways to succeed

* Never stop learning, for successful people, every day is a learning day. You see, learning does not necessarily have to be in a class room and the more you expose yourself to activities outside your cocoon, the more you will learn.

* Believe in your ability to reach your success no matter what.

* Maintain a positive mental attitude that allows you to sustain in the face of adversity and hardships

* Let no feeling of discouragement overcome your drive to succeed

*Be determined to work hard and smart and not to back down. Success is not just like a fruit you pluck on the tree. It takes time for the tree to grow and produce the fruits. So, buckle up!

* Above all, get off your couch and take massive actions, the actions that will propel you in the direction of your success.

* Know that success is a choice and not wishful thinking. You must want it. You must work for it. You must say no to distractions.

Let me give you an example, when I was raising three kids as a single mother, working full time, and going to school full time that was my choice. If I didn't make that choice, I would have lived on the minimum wage or perhaps depended upon government assistance. Because I chose to work hard and decided to become a nurse, I was able to endure sleepless nights, no fun times with friends. Some friends judged me because I was always busy and I had to put my kids in day care. What is your success causing you to miss? Anyone who has ever accomplished anything worthwhile had to give up something to gain success. You make that choice, not your parents, friends, time or even money. As Anthony Robbins said "it's not the lack of resources, it's your lack of resourcefulness that stops you."

"If you do what you've always done, you'll get what you've always gotten." –Tony Robbins

> *"Life takes on meaning when you become motivated, set goals and charge after them in an unstoppable manner"*
> *–Les Brown*

You can't build your success if you do not know what it looks like. As Stephen Covey said in his book *The 7 Habits of Highly Effective People*, "begin with the end in mind. Can you imagine what your future looks like, how much money you want to make, what kind of house you want to live in, how many lives you want to change, what kind of life partner, cars, where you want to vacation. Can you create a clear blueprint?

> *"People with clear, written goals, accomplish far more in a shorter period of time than people without them could ever imagine." – Brian Tracy*

Have you written your goals down? That is the first step to achieving them.

If you have not written your goals and do not have them outside of your head, then you have not decided yet. You are basically daydreaming and fantasizing. I will write that book one day. I will get a better job one day. I will lose weight someday. I will share my passion with the world one day. Do you see where this is going? How many times have you seen someone doing the things you always wanted to do and you had to look the other way and tell yourself "I just don't have the time now"? "I will do it soon!" As Tony Robbins said "It is in your moments of decision that your destiny is shaped."

If you do not have clarity in your decision, then find the answers; seek out from people who are knowledgeable in the field you are trying to master. If you want to become an accountant find an accountant to mentor you. I once came across this wonderful quote from Tony Robbins "Quality questions create a quality life. Successful people ask better questions, and as a result, they get better answers." Clarity creates focus which leads to success.

Are you holding back from becoming the person you are meant to be because you are afraid of what others will say about you?

"Other people's opinion of you does not have to become your reality." - Les Brown
"Life has no limitations, except the ones you make."
—Les Brown

Chapter 15

ROAD TO RESILIENCE

Love and Connections: You need to develop outstanding relationship with close family, friends and your community. Always learn to serve others.

See Crises as Opportunity to Grow: You can't change what happens, but you can change how you view and respond to these events. Use these setbacks or hardships as new opportunities to grow and become more resilient

Change is a part of living: You need to accept the circumstances but whatever you do, do not quit on your goals. Change your approach but never change your goals. If one road closes, try another one.

Laser focus: Have clarity on your goals. Take an action toward your goals daily. Celebrate the small victories "What's one thing I know I can accomplish today that will help me move in the direction I want to go?"

Take massive actions. Take decisive actions, rather than detaching completely from problems, stress and wishing they would just go away. Never back down from a challenge because of fear, take the leap and face it head on.

Self-discovery: How are you growing? What books are you reading?   What seminar are you attending? Who is your mentor? What have you learned about yourself through your latest challenge?

Nurture yourself: Who is filling your cup? How are you taking care of your mental health? Are you exercising? Are you meditating? What is your diet like? Are you developing confidence in your ability to solve problems and trusting your instincts so that you can become resilient?

Radiate positive outlook. Be an optimist and create positivity around you, this will enable you to attract great things in life. You must see things better than they are, visualizing what you want, rather than worrying about what you fear.

"The path to success is to take massive, determined action."
– Tony Robbins

Despite the hardships, I encountered while growing up, there is no place for hatred in my heart other joy and happiness.

What is happiness? Happiness is repeated countless times throughout our life; a word, so important that people will give their last sweat to achieve it. What happiness is and is not, depends upon our understanding of the true happiness, a happiness for no apparent reason where you can have any emotion—including sadness, fear, anger, or hurt—but you still experience that underlying state of peace and well-being. What defines and shapes our mood lies in the way we choose to view our existence and the events around us.

When I was growing up I went through a lot of difficulties, and at that time, I understood that I can create my own happiness whether I was experiencing negative or positive occurrences in my life. I could not overlook my problems, hide them under a blanket, give personal interpretations to them and pretend they have never happened. I tried it and failed many times that I can count. I came to the realization that it was not fixing my problem and my ability to be happy was based on external occurrences. Though I could easily smile but I was not inwardly happy.

Happiness is not synonymous of feeling good and pretending to overlook the negative feeling. Have you heard someone saying I will be happy when I find that perfect boyfriend/ girlfriend, job or degree, but what happen when we get those things? Likely that moment of euphoria has disappeared and now we are looking for another source of happiness. Happiness is not a mile stone or a miracle pill. It is understanding that you are in control of your life. How you think determines how you feel and controls the level of happiness in your life. Therefore, getting a grip on your emotions and thought process is crucial to creating happiness and fulfillment in your life. You need not to deny the negative aspects of certain situations, but look for the opportunities in those challenges.

*Do you want to achieve a deep sense of personal clarity and direction?

*Pay attention to your thoughts and do not deny them.

*Learn to understand and manage your emotions.

*Cultivate your mind and change your view point; don't focus what may be good or bad. Your interpretation is what makes it good and bad.

*Don't run away from negative thoughts, acknowledge them.

*Radiate your positive attitude to others and be the change you wish to see.

*Take personal responsibility for your actions and understand that no one can make you HAPPY. It is only you that can create your happiness!

Our happiness depends on our ability to respond in a manner that supports our highest values. The obvious truth is that as long as you put the blame on someone else for your life circumstances, you will have a hard time discovering the happiness in you. Yes, things have occurred to me that I wanted to accuse my grandmother, my uncle Abdi, my mother, my father; but at the end of the day, if I dwelled in that state of mind, how could I and can I discover my own happiness and bring it out. As Marci Shimoff said "you bring happiness to your outer experiences rather than trying to extract happiness from them".

The aptitude to respond to things that happen in our life –however we may define it- drastically affects our happiness. The happiest people respond to the situations that have occurred in their life in a way that corroborates their inner peace and well-being.

It is important to identify negative feelings without denying them in order to develop strategies to deal with them and reach the happiness set-point in our life:

-focusing on the fact and embrace your thoughts and feelings and being in the "now" moment

- Connect your blueprints with your highest values

- Make a firm decision to take massive actions.

A magnet is made of the positive and negative poles. You can't always overlook the negative thoughts and feelings but rather embrace them all, and then focus on the positive ones. We need to move beyond self-limiting thoughts and emotions so we can obtain, express and enjoy our values.

Practice:

1. Acceptance: Painful and unpleasant thoughts can be alleviated by identifying them and acknowledging them. Do not suppress or deny them. Create some distance by saying "I'm having the thought that …" And in doing so, you put some distance between the thought and yourself. In other words, we strive for objectivity.

2. Extension: welcoming those unpleasant thoughts and feelings in order to efficiently deal with them.

3. Embrace: being fully aware of your present moment.

4. Make a clear distinction between your thoughts and observations and focus on observing yourself.

5. Values: Who are you? What is your purpose in life? What kind of person are you and do you want to be? What is significant and meaningful to you?

6. Get excited and take a massive action. You are in control of your destiny, you can create your happiness, take that first step and follow up with that commitment to excellence and your life will not be the same.

Bibliography

U.S. Department of State, Diplomacy in Action. September 26, 2011. Bureau of African Affairs: Somalia.
http:;//www.state.gov/r/pa/ei/bgn/2863.htm

Dadaab: The World's Biggest Refugee Camp Al Jazeera, 11 July 2011.
http://english.aljazeera.net/indepth/features/2011/0 7/201171182844876473.htm.

The Boolean 2011: Dadaab a Forgotten City in the 21st Century (Damien McSweeny)

Somalia – History; Encyclopedia of the Nations.
http://www.nationsencyclopedia.com/Africa/Somali a-HISTORY.html

International Medical Corps.
Http://internationalmedicalcorps.org.

27412246R00103

Made in the USA
Lexington, KY
04 January 2019